ENGLISH TO GURKHALI DICTIONARY

ENGLISH TO GURKHALI DICTIONARY

A. W. CORNELIUS

GYAN

Published by

Gyan Publishing House
5, Ansari Road
Daryaganj, New Delhi-110002
Phone: 011-47034999, 9811692060
E-mail: books@gyanbooks.com

Distribution Network
gyanbooks.com
India, USA, Canada, UK, Australia, France

ISBN : 978-81-212-4313-1 (PB)

2nd Impression 2020

Printed at: Gyan Press, Delhi.

English to Gurkhali Dictionary
Author: A. W. Cornelius

HEAD QUARTERS, MEERUT DIST,

DEHRA DUN.

31st December, 1942.

This is to certify that Mr. A. W. Cornelius has been employed by this District as an Army Language Teacher. He is a very experienced Urdu Instructor, extremely conscientious and thorough in all his work. We have received excellent testimonials about his good work from the officers he has instructed in Dehra Dun. I can thoroughly recommend him as a first-class Munshi.

In Dehra Dun, Mr. Cornelius has instructed in addition to numerous individual officers, classes at the following Units *5/2nd Gurkha Rifles*, *5/9th Gurkha Rifles*, *107th British General Hospital* and at the *Survey of India*. They are all extremely satisfied with his work.

G. J. FOLKARD
MAJOR—A. E. C.
For Major General
Commander, Meerut District.

PREFACE

to

"THE ENGLISH TO GURKHALI DICTIONARY"

The present volume was originally intended as a Companion to the "*European Guide to Gurkhali*" written by me.

I have tried to avoid the use of Hindi words, when a Nepali word was available. Nothing has been left undone to make the work easy to *British Officers*. *Khaskhura* has been used in this book, which is the most common language of the inhabitants of Nepal.

My best thanks are due to A. Sada, Esqr., 3rd Gurkha Centre, Dehra Dun.

I owe a heavy debt of gratitude to Capt. Hulse, 2nd Gurkha Centre, Dehra Dun. It is due, in a large measure, to his kindness and encouragement that the present work has been composed and printed.

All future help and suggestions will be appreciated by the Author.

Permanent Address:—

A. W. CORNELIUS,
73, Chitwapur Road,
Lucknow, U. P.

March, 1944.

Abbreviations

Trans	—	for Transitive Verb
Int	—	for Intransitive Verb
Adj	—	„ Adjective
Adv	—	„ Adverb
n	—	„ Noun
g	—	„ Garnu—to do
h	—	„ Hunnu—to be
f	—	„ Feminine
v	—	„ Verb

The Long Vowels

á (long) is like English "a" in Army, pass, father

í (long) is „ „ "i" „ Police, machine

ú (long) „ „ „ "u" „ Rule, too

e (long) „ „ „ "e" „ Say, belly, fate, pay

o (long) „ „ „ "o" „ Old, rope, go

The Short Vowels

a (short) is like English "a" in Woman, apart

i (short) „ „ „ "i" „ Bill, kiss

u (short) „ „ „ "u" „ Full, pull

A

Absccss ... Pilo (f)
Able ... Saknu
Above ... Uṉbho, máṉthi
Absent ... Gail, bihájir
Abundance ... Dherai, parasastai
Abuse ... Gálí
Account ... Hisáb, Hisáp
Accident ... Saṉyog, wáqá
Accord ... Ichchhá
Accusation ... Dosh
Accurate ... Ṭhík
Acid ... Khatto
Acknowledge ... Mánnu
Ache (to) ... Dukhnu
Acquaintance ... Chinejáne, Chinájáni,
Act (to) ... Kám garnú
Acquit ... Chhoṛi diṉnú
Acre ... Bíghá, ropni
Across ... Wárí, pári
Advance (money) ... Pesgí
Add (to) ... Joṛnu
Address ... Ṭhegáná, patá
Adhere (to) ... Ṭásnu
Admonition ... Chetanne
Adult ... Ṭhulo

Adornment	... Gahaná
Adze	... Bachhilá, báṉsulá
Afford	... Dinu
Afraid of	... Dekhi ḍaráuṉnu
Afraid (to be)	... Darnu, jhasang, hunnu
Afternoon	... Sáṉjh
After	... Pachhi
Afterwards	... Pachhi
Again	... Pherí
Against	... Biruddha
Age	... Umar, umer
Agree	... Ráji, łau bhanṇu,
Agreement	... Lekhá patrí
Ago	... Bhayo
Aim (to)	... Táknu
Air	... Hawá, batás
Alligator	... Guhí, sus,
Allow	... Dinu
Alert	... Chanákho
All	... Sabai, (sab)
Alms	... Dán
Alike	... Eknáse, barábar
Alive	... Jiuṉdai, jiuṉdo
Also	... Paní
Aloud	... Charko
Alone	... Eklai
Alter	... Phernu, badalnu

Along ... Láṉmai tira, báṭo, saṉgmá
Already ... Paile, aghi nai
Alphabet ... Kakhará, akshar
Alternately ... Pálai pálo
Altogether ... Sáṉṭṭhai, sabai
Always ... Sadhaiṉ, barábar
Amend ... Sáṭo
Ammunition ... Bárud golí
Amuse ... Ramáunu
Amidst ... Májh má
Amount ... Jamá
Ambush ... Lukne tháuṉ, ghá,
Ancestor ... Jiju báje
And ... Aru, ani, ra, ta
And so ... Pheri
Anger ... Rís, risáuṉnu
Ankle ... Golí gánṭhá, guligánṭha
Animal ... (Jantu), pashu, (pasu,)
Angle ... Kuṉna, kuná
Angry (to get) ... Risháunu
Annoy (to) ... Khijyauṉnu, khijánu khisi garnu
Anoint ... Ghasnu, telia chakar
Ant (white) ... Dhuniro
Ant ... Kamilo
Anvil ... Líhí
Another ... Árko

Answer, back (to)	...	Mukh joṛnu
Answer, (an)	...	Uttar, juwáp
Any	...	Koi, kei, kunai
Antelope	...	Mirg
Anxiety	...	Surtá, shok
Any where	...	Kahíṉ pani
Any how	...	Kastai gari pani
Anything	...	Kei pani
Ape, (an)	...	Dheruwá
Apologize	...	Máphi máṉgnu
Apology	...	Máph "
Apparatus	...	Tánábáná
Apparently	...	Dekhnyá gari
Appearance (of a person)	...	Rúp
Appeal	...	Doháí, arji
Apple	...	Sew, seo
Appetite	...	Bhok
Appoint	...	Khaṭáuṉnu
Application	...	Arjí patra
Apply	...	Lagáuṉnu
Appointment	...	Kám páunu
Approach	...	Pugnu lágnu
April	...	Baisákh
Apricot	...	Khumáni
Apprehend	...	Pakrannu
Archer	...	Guleli khelne, dhanudhári

Arm (upper	...	Paṉkhṛá,
fore)	...	háth
Approval	...	Maṉjúri
Arch	...	Dhanurúpí, sirán
Armourer	...	Kami, lohár
Area	...	Haṭṭá
Army	...	Palṭan (fauj)
Armpit	...	Kákhí
Argue	...	Bibád
Arouse	...	Uṭháunu, Binjaunu
Arithmetic	...	Hisáp
Around	...	Cháraitira
Arms	...	Hatiyár haru
Arrange	...	Thík párnu, sajyaunu
Arrest	...	Pakaṛṉnu
Arrive (at)	...	Pugnu, samma
Arrears	...	Báṉkí
Arrow	...	Kár
As many as	...	Jati sakdo
As soon as	...	Bittikai
As	...	Jasto, jhaiṉ, gari, jaso
As far as (I can)	...	Mero sakdobhar
Ask	...	Sodhnu
Ascend	...	Chaṛhnu, ukalnu
Ashes	...	Kharáni
Aside	...	Eká paṭṭi
Ascent	...	Ukálo

Ass	... Gadahá, gadalú, (f)
Assistance	... Madadgár, gohárе
Assessment	... Sirtu
Assort	... Rakam
Astride	... Goṛá pasárí, ghuṉṛá
Assist	... Gohár g, (dhásere
Ashamed (of)	... Sharmáunu
Ashamed, (to be)	... Dekhí
Ashamed (of)	... Laz lágiáko, laz manniako
Ask (demand)	... Máṉgnu sodhnu
Assault	... Maṉthí ái lágnu, máṉrpịt g,
Assemble	... Thuprinu
Assets	... Jaujat
Astronomer	... Jotishi
Attempt	... (Mihnat), mihnit
Attend	... Sundai rahaṉnu
Attack, (to)	... Chhopnu, larnu
Attack, (n)	... Dháwá
Attend (watch)	... Herdai rahaṉnu
Aunt	... Phupu, jeṭhi ámá, kánchhi ámá, phuphi
Auction	... Lílám
Authority	... Aktiyár
August	... Bhádao
Average	... Ausat
Avenge	... Badalá linu

Away ... Ṭárá
Awl ... Sutárí
Awake ... (Int)—jágnu
... (Tran) jagáuṉnu
Awkward ... Lothro
Axle ... Dhurí, (dandá)
Axe ... Bancharo.

B

Baby ... Nàní
Bad ... Buro, najáti, narámro
Back ... Kanḍo, piṭh
Bachelor ... Kuwárá
Badge, (of rank) ... Billá
(distinction) ... Chino
Bag ... Thailo,—(sack—borá)
Bait ... Cháro
Baggage ... Sárdám, jhitimiṭi
Bag and baggage ... Kumlosumlo
Bake, (to) ... Seknu, (cook-polnu)
Bald ... Khuilo
Bail ... Jamáni
Balance ... Tulo, tarájú
" (remainder) ... Bánki
" (accounts) ... Hisáp miláuṉnu
Balcony ... Pidi
Balloon ... Gobára

Ball	... Gín, golí
Bale	... Kumlo
Band	... Bandhan
Bamboo	... Báṉs
Banana	... Kerá
Banker	... Sáhu
Bank, (earth)	... Ḍhiská
" (river)	... Pákhá, chheo, tír
Bankrupt	... Phakírí
Bar (gate)	... Tagáro
" (wood)	... Áglo
" (rod)	... Ghárá
Barber	... Náí, hazám
Barbed	... Káṉṛe
Bare, (adj)	... Naṉgá
Bare headed	... Muṛilo
Bare-foot	... Náṉgá goṛáko
Bark, (to)	... Bhuknu
" (tree)	... Bokrá
Barrel, (n)	... Pípá
" (of rifle)	... Nál
Barren	... Báṉjhí
" (land)	... Rukho
Barley	... Jau
Basket	... Ḍoko, korká, thunse
" (small)	... Ḍálo, ṭokarí
Basin	... Chilímchí

Basement	...	Bhúintalá
Bat, (bird)	...	Chamero
Bathing	...	Asnán, nuhái, (snán)
Bathe	...	Nohánu
Batch	...	Ṭoli, gaṭṭá
Be, (to)	...	Hunnu
Be awake	...	Biunjhinnu
Be wet	...	Bhijnu
Bean	...	Simí
Beam (small)	...	Bolo
" (big)	...	Dalín
Bear	...	Bhálu
Beat, (to)	...	Hánnu, márnu, birkáunu
Beard	...	Ḍárhí, ḍári
Beat, (to)	...	Píṭnu, (game) ṭhaṭák ṭhuṭuk g.
Bed	...	Káth
" (to make)	...	Bichháunu
Beauty	...	Rup
Beautiful	...	Rámro
Become, (to)	...	Hunnu
Because	...	Kinakí
Bee	...	Máuri
Before	...	Pahilo, agline, aghári
Bedding	...	Ochchhyán
Beetle	...	Gobáre, kirá
Behind	...	Pachháṛí, pachhí

Begin, (to)	... Lágnu, shuru garnu, thálnu
Beggar	... Bhikári
Belly	... Peṭ, bhúṉṛi
Belong	... Huṉnu
Behaviour	... Chalan
Below	... Tala, úṉdhọ, muni
Bellows	... Bhánṭi, khaláti, ágo
	... phukne
Believe, (to)	... Patyáunu
Bell	... Ghaṉṭí
Beseech	... Binti g.
Bend, (to)	... Mornu, khuncháunu
Bent	... Ghobṭo
Bend over, (to)	... Níuranu
Besiege	... Gheri, basnu
Besides	... Upránta, báhik
Beside	... Paṭṭi, chheu, nira
Beyond	... Pallo patti
Between	... Bhittra, bích, máṉjha
Best	... Játi, assal
Bid	... Hukm
" ,(offer)	... Dák bolnu
Big	... Ṭhulo
Bill	... Hisáb, exchange, huṉḍi
Bird	... Chará, paṉchhí
Bitter	... Títo

Birth	... Jaṉma
Bit	... Kareli, tukrá
Bite, (to)	... Ṭoknu, kháṉnu
Blacksmith	... Kámi, (lohár)
Blast	... Suruṉ hánnu
Black	... Kálo
Blade, (knife)	... Dhár
Blanket	.. Kámlo, pákhi, ráṛi
Blame	... Dosh
Blemish	... Khoṭ
Blessing	.. Ásis
Blind	... Aṉdha, aṉdho
" (one eyed)	... Kááná
Blight	... Rátopaheṉlo
Blister	... Phoká
Blink	... Chimchim
Blood	... Ragat
Blossom	... Pos
Blockhead	... Laṭheprá
Blotting paper	... Sosnyá kágaj
Blow out, (to)	... Nibháuṉnú
Blow, (fist)	... Ghussá, muṛki
Blow, (n)	... Hirkáí
Blow, (wind)	... Bahaṉnu
Blow, (to)	... Phukṉu
Blush, (to)	... Láj ánu
Blue	.. Nilo

Blunt	.. Na lágne, bodho
Boat	.. Ḍuṉgá
Boar	.. Banel
Board	... Phalyák
Body	.. Sarír, áng, júi
Bog	.. Simsár, dháp, hilchhúiṉ
Bomb	.. Bamgolá
Bold	.. Ántilo, karántilo
Boil, (to)	.. Usinnu, Unglnu, Umálnu
Boil, (noun)	.. Pilo
Bolt, (door)	.. Áglo, chhiṭkani
Bond	.. Hátchiṭṭhá
Bonus	.. Bakshiprápli
Boot	.. Juttá
Bone	.. Háṛ
Book	.. Pustak, kitáp
Book-keeping	.. Lekhájokha
Boot-maker	.. Sárki
Bore (to)	.. Chheṉṛnu
Border, (country)	.. Dosán
Born, (to be)	.. Janmaṉnu
Both	.. Dinta, duwai
Bottom	.. Tala, tháh, puchhár
Borrow, (to)	.. Riṉ liṉnu
Bow, (n)	.. Dhanu
Bow, (to)	.. Dhok
Box	.. Sampaṭ, (bákas)

Boy	.. Chhoro, ketá
Bowl, (n)	.. Batuko
Braces	.. Gálich
Bracelet	.. Churá, bálá
" seller	.. Churáti
Brass	. Pítal
Bran	.. Chokar
Brain	. Gidi
Brand	.. Agulṭhe
Branch, (n)	.. Háṉgá
Bravery	.. Ánṭ
Brave	.. Bír ántilo
Bread	.. Roṭí
Break, (to)	.. Tornu, phornu, báṉchnu
Breath	.. Sáns linu
Breadth	.. Gaj
Breast	.. Chháti
Brick	.. Ìṉṭá, inta
Brick-layer	.. Gárokarnú
Bribe	.. Ghus
Bride-groom	.. Dulhá, beulá
Bride	.. Dulhání, beulí
Bridle	.. Kareli
Brim	.. Nimtho
Brittle	.. Jhuro
Bridge	.. Sángo, Sánhu, pool.
Broad	.. Gajílo, cháklo, moto

Brown .. Khairo

Broom .. Kucho

Brother .. Dáju

Bud .. Kopílá

Bucket .. Ḍoṭho

Buffalo .. Bhaiṉsi

.. Ráṉgo

Bug .. Uṛus

Bugle .. Bikul

Build, (to) .. Banáunu

Bulb .. Dallá

Bull .. Sáṉṛ goru

Bullet .. Golí

Bullock .. Goru

Bundle .. Gaṭṭhá, biṭá

Bunch .. Jhuppá

Burn, (to) .. Jalnu, palnu ḍaṛnu

Burden .. Bhárí

Bury, (to) .. Purnu, Gáṛnu

Burglar .. Ghar phorne

Burst, (to) .. Phutnu

Bush .. Jhor, pothra,

Busy .. Lágyeko

Business .. Kám

Butcher .. Kąsái

Butter .. Makkhan, ghiu,

But .. Tara

Butterfly	... Putli
Butt, (gun)	... Kunjá, kundá
Butts	... Gumti
Button	.. Tánk
Buttock	... Chak
By-way	... Charbáṭo
By	.. Le
Buy, (to)	.. Kinnu

C

Cabbage	.. Gabí
Cage	.. Pinjaro
Calf	.. Báchchho
" (leg)	.. Tikhra
Call	.. Ḍáknu, boláuṉnu
Calm	.. Sunsán
Camp	.. Paṛáo, (bás)
Camel	.. Uṉṭ
Can, (v)	.. Saknu, (n) ghaṛá
Cane	.. Bet
Cannon	.. Top
Candle	.. Mom-battí
Canal	... Kulo
Cantonment	.. Chháoní
Capsize, (to)	.. Lotaunu
Cap	.. Ṭopí
Carcase—(animal)	.. Siṉnu

Cardamoms	.. Alainchi
Card	.. Tás
Care	.. Phikar, (jimmá)
Carpet	.. Darí
Careful	.. Khabardár
Careless	.. Bearthai
Carry, (to)	.. Boknu.
Carpenter	.. Baṛhaí, káṭhkarmi
Carriage	.. Baggí, gáṛí,
Carrot	.. Gájar
Cart	.. Gáṛí
Cash	.. Nakhati
Caste	.. Ját
Cask	.. Pípá
Cast, (to)	... Hálnu
Castrated–(v)	.. Khasi
Cat	.. Birálo
Cattle	.. Gáí, goru
Catch, (to)	.. Pakrannu
Cause	.. Káran
Cauliflower	.. Phulgopi
Cavalry	.. Risála, bruksawár
Cave	.. Orár
Cement	.. Biláití maṭṭí
Ceiling	.. Chhánná
Cellar	.. Bhaṭṭí
Cemetery	.. Chihán

Certain	... Sán̲chai, phaláná
Certainly	... Nisse
Ceremony	... Tíwár
Census	... Nán̲ulekhái
Chaff	... Bhús, bhúso
Chair	... Chaukí, kursí
Chalk	... Kharyá
Chain	... Sikri, jhimjiri, Sánglo
Challenge	... Laṛáín̲,
(sentry)	... Paharshabda mán̲gnu,
Chance,	
(opportunity)	... Belá, mauká
" (to)	... Sanyog
Change	... (Money) rejí
"	... Phernu sánṭnu
Character	... Chál chalan
Charcoal	... Koilá, angár
Charge (enemy)	... Hamla
Charge, (care)	... Sonpí
Charge (cost)	... Dám
(accussation)	... Phirát
Charm	... Mantra
Charity box	... Dán
Chatter	... Kachkachia, gangania
Cheap	... Sasto
Cheat, (to)	... Ṭhagnu, dhántnu, chhalnu

Cheerful	...	Khushí
Cheery	...	Payán
Cheek	...	Gálá, gala
" (to)	...	Gijáunu
Cheese	...	Panír
Chesnut	...	Pángrá
Chess	...	Satrang
Chew, (to)	...	Chabáuṉnu
Chicken-pox	...	Kánkará, mái ko bimárí
Chief	...	Mukhiá
Chicken	...	Challá, kukhro
Child	...	Bálakha, náni
Children	...	Lálábálà, keṭáketí
Childless	...	Aputá
Chimney	...	Angeṭhí
Chisel	...	Chhiná
Chin	...	Chiúṉro
Chips	...	Lobṛá
Cholera	...	Haiza
Choose	...	Chhánnu, channu
Church	...	Girjá
Cinnamon	...	Sinkaulí
Circumference	...	Gherá
City	...	(Shahr), sahar
Cistern	...	Kúp
Class	...	Darja
Clay	...	Máṉṭo

Claim	...	Dáwá
Clean	...	Chokko
Clever	...	Sipalu, chalakí
Climb, (to)	...	Chaṛhnu
Climate	...	Háwá pání
Clock	...	Ghaṛí
Close	...	Band garnu
Clothes	...	Luga
Cloth	...	Kapará
Cloud	...	Bádal
Coal	...	Patthar ká koilá
Coarse	...	Báklo
Coin	...	Reji
Coir	...	Nariwalko nasá
Cold	...	Chiso
Cold (n)	...	Jáṛo
" (disease)	...	Ruga, sardí
Collect	...	Jama garnu
Colour	...	Rang
Come	...	Áu
Come, (to)	...	Áuṉnu, (or awnu)
Command,	...	Hukum dinu
Commence (to)	...	Thainu, shuru
Commencement	...	Shuru
Comment	...	Rai dinu
Commerce	...	Baipár yá beopár
Commodity	...	Mál, jins

Common	... Mamulí
Commonly	... Mamuli garí
Common sense	... Samajh
Communication	... Hál khabar
Companion	... Sáthi
Company	... Sátha
Compare	... Barábarí, milái hernu
Compared, (to)	... Tulná garnu
Comparision	... Tulná
Compartment (Railway)	... Ḍibba
Compass	... Kampás
Compel, (to)	... Abasse lagáuṉnu
Compensation	... Harjána
Complaint, (n)	... Shikáyat
Complete, (to)	... Saknu, purá garnu
Complete, (adj)	... Khatam garnu
Completely	... Púrai
Complexion	... Lubhán
Complicate	... Mushkil
Compliments	... Salám
Compound	... Misyá ko
Comprehension	... Samajh
Compromise	... Ráji námá
Compulsory	... Jaruri
Compulsion	... Bhár
Comrade	... Sáthi saṉgi

Conceal, (to)	...	Ḍháṉknu
Concealment	...	Chhupáo
Concentrate, (attention)	...	Dhyán jamánu
Concern	...	Sambaṉdh
Concession	...	Riyáyat
Conclude, (to)	...	Natijá nikálnu
Condemn, (stuff)		Kharáb garnu
Condemn, (to) (court of law)	...	Doshi ṭharánu
Condiment	...	Masálá
Condition	...	Hálat, gat, paṉ
Conduct, (n)	...	Chál chalan
Conduct, (to)	...	Chaláuṉnu
Confectioner	...	Miṭhái wálá
Confess	...	Káel h, máṉnu
Confidence	...	Bishwás
Confuse	...	Phark kaunu
Conquer, (to)	...	Jitnu
Conquest	...	Jít
Consequence	...	Natijá
Consider, (to)	...	Bichárnu
Constantly	...	Barábar
Contribution	...	Madad
Contrary	...	Ultáulo
Control	...	Rok
Continue	...	Gardai jánu

Continuous	... Nirantar
Converse, (to)	... Bolnu
Conveyance	... Sawárí
Convict, (to)	... Ṭhahranu
Convict	... Aprádhi
Convince, (to)	... Bishwás garánú
Cook, (to)	... Pakáunu
Cook	... Bawarchi, bhansí
Cook house	... Bhánsaghar, chulo
Cooking-pot	... Bhánrá
Cool	... Chiso
Coolie	... Bhariya
Copy, (to)	... Sárnu
Cope with, (to)	... Nipaṭnu
Copious	... Jiyáda
Copy, (imitate)	... Nakal párnu
Copper	... Támba
Copper-smith	... Bánṛá
Cork	... Birko
Corn	... Ánáj
Corns	... Khílí
Corner	... Kuná
Corporal	... Náik, (corporal)
Corpse	... Murdá
Correct, (to)	... Lagát ká dám
Cost	... Dám
Cost, (to)	... Dám lagnu

Cost price ... Kharid ko dám
Cotton ... Kapás
Cotton cloth ... Sutí kapṛá
Cough, (n) ... Khokí
Counsel ... Salláh
Count, (to) ... Gannu
Counter attack, (to) ... Counter attack garnu
Counted, (3rd plu)... Ganye
Country ... Des
Coup ... Chhápa márnu
Couple ... Joṛá
Couple, (to) ... Joṛ dinu
Courage ... Sáhas, dhiraj
Course ... Rastá
Court yard ... Ágan
Courteous ... Dayálu
Cousin ... Bhatija, (bhánjá)
Cover, (lid) ... Ḍhakkan
Cover ... Áṛ
Cover, (to) ... Chhopnu, dháknu
Covering fire ... Covering fire
Cow ... Gáí
Coward ... Káfar, ḍarpok
Cow-dung ... Gobar
Cowherd ... Gwála
Cowshed ... Goṭh

Crab	.. Gangathá
Crack	.. Phúṭ
Crack, (to)	.. Phúṭnu
Cradle	.. Kokro
Cramp, to (get)	.. Akṛinu
Cramped	.. Akṛya ko
Crazy	.. Págal
Cream	.. Kuráni
Crease, (to)	.. Dobriánu
Crease	.. Dobri
Creditor	.. Sáhú
Creek	.. Kaṛí
Creep, (to)	.. Gasari gasari jánu
Creeper, (n)	... Lahara
Crime	.. Aparádh, páp
Criminal	.. Pápí, aprádhí
Cringe	.. Nidre garnu
Cripple	.. Lulo
Crisis	.. Najuk waqt
Crocodile	.. Gúhi, (sus), ghaṛiyál
Crockery	.. Chinimaṭṭi ko bhán̲da
Crooked	.. Bhángo
Crop	.. Fasal
Cross	.. Pári jan̲nu
Cross	.. Áṛá, tirchho
Cross examine	.. Sawál káṭnu
Cross legged	.. Paleti marera, basanu

Cross roads	..	Chaurástá
Crow	..	Kág
Crowbar	..	Jhampal, sábal, sabbal
Crowd	..	Ghuchho
Crowded, (to be)	..	Ghuchho h
Crown	..	Táj
Crown	..	Mukut
Crude	..	Kachcha
Cruel	..	Nisṭhur
Cruelty	..	Nirdai
Crush, (to)	..	Michnu, ṭhokar lagnu
Cry, (call out)	..	Karáunu
Cry, (to)	..	Runu, karaunu
Cub	..	Bachcha
Cuckoo	..	Kuku chara
Cucumber	..	Kánkro
Culprit	..	Doshi
Cultivate, (to)	..	Kamaunu
Cultivator	..	Kisáni
Cultivation	..	Khetipáti
Cunning	..	Chalák
Cup	..	Baṭuko, (Kaṭorá)
Curly	..	Ghungari, Ghumáyáko
Curl, (to)	..	Ghumaunu
Curtain	..	Pardá
Curry	..	Tyun
Custom	..	Rítí, báni

Customer .. Gáhaki
Cut, (to) .. Káṭnu
Cutting, (of plant).. Kalam
Cymbals .. Manjurí

D

Dacoit .. (Chor). ḍákú
Dacoity .. Ḍáka
Dagger .. Chupi, Chepsa
Daily .. Dinahúṉ, roj roj
Dam .. Bánd
Damage ... Nuksán, nás
Damaged ... Kharáb huṉnu
Damages .. Harjána
Dance, (to) .. Náchnu
Dancing place ... Rodí
Danger .. Bhayanak, ḍár, jokhim, (jagjagi)
Dangerous .. Khatarnák, ápat ko
Daring .. Himmat
Daring, (a) .. Diler
Dark .. Aṉdhyáro
Darkness .. Andhyáro
Dart, (to) .. Jhapaṭnu
Dash against, (to) .. Jor le lagnu
Dasera, (festival) .. Dasai
Date .. Tithi, bár

Date, (fruit)	... Khajúr
Daughter	... Chhorí
Dawn	... Bihána prátai, rumi ujel
Day	... Din
Day before yesterday	... Asti
Day after tomorrow	... Parsi
Day break, at	... Bholi, (din nikle)
Day light, in	... Diun̲so
Day time	... Diun̲so
Day and night	... Rát din
Dead	... Mareko, Man̲ryeko
Deadlock	... Thám
Deaf	... Bhairo, (bairo)
Dear, (beloved)	... Priya, (piyáro)
Dear, (expensive)	... Mahan̲go
Dearness	... Mahan̲gái
Dearth	... Kamí
Death	... Mṛityu, kál
Debility	... Kamjorí
Debt	... Rin̲
Debtor	... Asámi
Deceit	... Dhokha
Deceive, (to)	... Dán̲ṭnu, ṭhagnu
Decide	... Ṭhahráun̲nu
Decision	... Tai

Decline, (to) ... Kam huna, ghaṭnu
December ... Pús
Decrease, (to) ... Ghaṭnu
Decrease, (n) ... Ghaṭí
Deduct, (to) ... Ghaṭáuṉnu
Deduction ... Ghaṭaeko
Deed, (action) ... Kám
Deep .. Gahíro
Deepen, (to) ... Gahiro garnu
Deer ... Mirga
Defeat, (n) .. Hár
Defeat, (to) ... Háráunu
Defeated, (to be) ... Háreko
Defence ... Uttar, Bachái, bacháwat
Defences ... Bachaunu
Defend ... Bachau
Deformed ... Kubro
Deficiency ... Apugdo, khacho
Defraud ... Dhokhá dínu
Degrade, (to) ... Darja ghaṭanu
Delay, (n) ... Abelá, biyáuṉlo
Delay ... Biyáuṉlo garnu
Delight ... Ánand, bhog
Deliver, (to) ... Páunu
Demolish ... Bhatkáuṉnu, bigarnu
Demon ... Bhút, deo
Deny .. Aswíkár g

Depart ... Chuṭinu
Descend, (to) ... Utrannu, or htánnu
Descend ... Tala ánu
Describe, (to) ... Bakharnu
Descent ... Orálo
Desert, (to) ... Bhágnu, retilo thaun
Deserve, (to) ... Rakhnu
Deserter ... Bhagaurá
Deserving ... Láik
Desirable ... Cháhíndo
Desire ... Bichár
Desolate ... Usar
Despair ... Asha na bhae ko
Despise ... Tuchchh ṭhánnu, hela
Destitute ... Harikangál
Detail, (to) ... (Khataunu) Deatail g
Detachment ... Kamán
Detain, (to) ... Roknu
Detect, (to) ... Pata lagánu
Development ... Unnati
Device ... Dhang
Devil ... Bhút
Devotee ... Bhagat
Dew ... Os, sit
Diagonally ... Chhatkyá
Diamond, (precious stone)... Hirá

Diamond, (cards) .. Inṭá
Diarrhoea .. Chheṛauṭi
Diary .. Dúdh ghar
Dice .. Pánsá
Did .. Gare
Die, (to) .. Bitnu, marnu, maṉrnu
Diet .. Khánu
Difference .. Bhed
Different .. Beglai, farak
Difficult .. Sáro, muskil
Difficulty .. Kaṭhin
Dig .. Khannu
Digest, (to) .. Pacháunu
Diligence .. Jatan, dástí
Diligent .. Dáste, jatane
Dine, (to) .. Chobnu
Dip, (to) .. Kháná khánu
Dirt .. Mailá
Direct, (to) .. Batlánu
Direction .. Tira, disa
Dirty .. Mailo, phori
Disadvantage .. Háni
Disappoint .. Áshámáṉrnu
Disapprove, (to) .. Narucháúnu
Disarm, (to) .. Hathiyár li linu
Discharge .. Nám káṭnu, náṉu katáuṉnu

Disciple	.. Shisye
Discipline	.. Shikshá, ainmanáí
Discover, (to)	.. Paunu
Discuss, (to)	... Bibad garnu
Disease	.. Rog, bimár, bethá
Disembark	.. Jaháj báṭa utarnu
Disengaged	.. Rito
Disgrace	.. Helá
Disgrace, (to)	.. Helá garnu
Disguise, (in)	.. Bhes badalnu
Dish	.. Thálí
Dishonest	.. Kapti, chhali, beimán
Dishonesty	.. Dhokhá
Dislike, (to)	.. Man na paraunu
Disloyal	.. Nimakharám
Disloyalty	.. Nimakharámi
Dismiss, (to)	.. Chhuṭnu, chhornu
Dismiss, (cause to be)	.. Chhuṭáunu
Dismissal	.. Chhuṭṭi
Dismount, (to)	.. Utarnu, jhaṛnu
Disobedience	.. Námanáí
Disobedient	.. Námánne
Disobey	.. Namannu
Disperse, (to)	.. Phailáunu phijáunu
Displease, (to)	.. Jhokáunu
Dispose, of (to)	.. Bechnu

Dispute, (n) ... Jhagrá
Distance ... Ṭáṛo
Distinct ... Sáf
Distant .. Ṭáṛo
Distribute, (to) ... Baṭnu
District ... Jilla
Disturb, (to) ... Gaṛbaṛánu
Disturbance .. Gulmale, dangá, háhu gulmul
Ditch, (drain) .. Kulo
Ditch, (pit) .. Kháṛal, khálto
Divide .. Bhág bhág, g, batnu
Diviner .. Jháṉkri
Divorce, (to) .. Chhutáunu, tyágnu
Dizziness .. Ringato
Dizzy .. Jiring jiring
Dizzy, (to be) .. Ringáunu
Do, (to) .. Garnu
Dock .. Jaháj ko tharne jágá
Doctor .. (Baidhi) Baidya
Doctrine .. Dheya
Doe ... Murlí
Dog, (wild) .. Boánso
Dog .. Kukur
Dog cart .. Kukur gáiṛi
Donkey .. Gadhá
Don't .. Na

Donor .. Dán dine wálá

Door .. Dailo

Doorway .. Dailo

Dose (of medicine) .. Mátrá

Double .. Doharo

Double up, (to) .. Duguṛnu

Doubt .. Shaṉká, (sakh)

Doubtless .. Abasse

Dough .. Khaṭṭo

Dove .. Parewa, dhukur

Down .. Tala, muntira, máklak

Down hill .. Orálo

Down stairs .. Tallo majil

Dowry .. Dáijo

Drain .. Kulo

Drain (stone) .. Mohorí

Draw, (to) .. Tánnu

Drawback .. Pachharitáiṉnu

Drawer .. Tannu

Drawing room .. Baiṭhak

Dream .. Sapaná

Dress .. Luga, pośhág

Dress, (to) .. Luga lagánu

Dress wound .. Paṭṭi báṉdhnu

Drink, (to) .. Piunu, (piuṉnu)

Drive, (to) .. Háṉknu

Drive into, (to) ..	Gáṛhnu
Drive away, (to) ..	Dhapáunu
Driver ...	Háṉkne wála
Drizzle ..	Jhimjhime
Drop, (n) ..	Thopo
Drop, (v. i.) ..	Chuhuṉnu
Dropsy ..	Peṭ phulne bimári
Drought ..	Obáno
Drown, (to) ..	Buṛnu, ḍubí márnu
Drowned, (to be) ..	Ḍubeko
Drudgery ..	Muskil ko kám
Druggist ..	Angreji dawái bechnewálá
Drum ..	Tambar
Drunk ..	Mátyeko
Drunkard ..	Matwálá, (matwál)
Drunkenness ..	Nasha
Dry ...	Sukye
Dry, (v.t) ..	Sukáuṉnu
Duck ..	Háns
Due ..	Karja
Dumb ..	Guṉgá
Dung ..	Mal
Dung, (human) ..	Gu
Dung, (cattle) ..	Gobar
During ..	Bhari
Dust ..	Dhúlo

Duster	..	Dhúlo jhárne kapṛá
Duty	..	Parne kám
Dwell, (to)	..	Rahnu
Dwelling	..	Basne jagá
Dye, (to)	..	Rangáunu
Dyer	..	Rangnewálá
Dynasty	..	Bans̱a
Dysentery	..	Ragalmáns̱í
Dyspepsia	..	Apach, (napache ko)

E

Each	..	Ek ek, janaṉge, goṭá
Each other	..	Ek dusra má
Eager	..	Ichchhuk
Eagle, (bird)	..	Garul, hárphori
Early	..	Bhayána
Early (in the morning)	..	Saberai, bhayána
Ear	..	Káṉn
Ear-ring	..	Kán ko mundro
Earn, (to)	..	Kamáuṉnu
Earnest	..	Baiṉná
" (in)	..	Sáchchi má
Earnings	..	Kamáí
Earth-quake	..	Bhuinchál
Earth	..	Pṛithibí

Earthen	.. Máṭo ko
Earth, (soil)	.. Máṉṭo, (bhiuṉko)
Earthen ware	.. Máṭo ko bháṉṛa
Ease	.. Sajílo
Easy	.. Sajilo gari
Easily	.. Sajílo
East	.. Púrab
Easy chair	.. Árám kursi
Eat, (to)	.. Kháṉnu
Eaves	.. Balení
Eclipse	.. Grahan
Economy	.. Kam karchi
Edge	.. Chheu
Edge, (knife)	.. Dhár
Edge, (river)	.. Kinará
Edge ways	.. Dhárilo
Education	.. Vidyá
Efficient	.. Láik
Effort	.. Jatan
Egg	.. Aṉdá, phul
Eight	.. Áṭh
Either (or)	.. Yo—arko
Eject, (to)	.. Nikáli dinu
Elder	.. Jetho, baṛo
Eldest	.. Sab bhanda ṭhulo
Elbow	.. Kuini
Elect, (to)	.. Chháṭnu

Electricity	.. Bijlí
Elephant	.. Háthí
Else, (a)	.. Arko
Elsewhere	.. Árko ṭháṉu
Embark, (to)	.. Jáháj má chaṛhnu
Embers	.. Ágo ko bhubro
Embrace, (to)	.. Angálo hálnu
Embroidery	.. Buṭá bharnu
Emerge, (to)	.. Niklnu
Emergency	.. Jaruri belá
Emperor	.. Mahárájá
Empty	.. Khálí
Encounter, (to)	.. Ámni sámni hunu.
End	.. Anta, khatam
Endurance	.. Parkhi
Endure, (to)	.. Parkhi janu
Enmity	.. Dushmaní
Enemy	.. Sattur, bairi, satru
Energy	.. Bal
Energetic	.. Mihnati
Enforce, (to)	.. Bal dinu, kám má lánu
Engage, (to)	.. Kám má lagánu
Engine	.. Kal
Enlist, (v. int)	.. Bhartí hunu
" (v. t.)	.. Bhartí garnu
Enlistment	.. Bhartí
Enough	.. Bhayo, dheraí

Enquire, (to)	..	Tháh garnu
Enrol, (to)	:	Bhartí garnu, nám lekháuṉnu
Enter, (to)	..	Pasnu, bhitra
Entreat, (to)	..	Bintí garnu
Entrails	..	Ándrá
Entrench, (to)	..	Morchábandi g
Entire	..	Sabai jati chha
Entrust, (to)	..	Jmmámáṉ rakhnu
Entangle, (to)	..	Aljhnu
Envelope	..	Lipҥápa
Envoy	..	Dút
Envy	..	Dáha
Epidemic	..	Sarne rog
Equal, (to)	..	Barábar h,
Equal	..	Barábar
Equip, (to)	..	Sajhyánu
Erase, (to)	..	Meṭnu
Eraser	..	Rubber
Erect	..	Ṭhaṛo
Erect, (to)	..	Lagánu, khaṛá garnu
Err, (to)	..	Bhúl g.
Error	..	Bhúl
Escape, (to)	..	Báṉchnu
Escape, (n)	..	Báṉchna
Escort	..	(Eskáuṭ), pahará
Especial	..	Mukhya

Especially	..	Assal garí
Espionage	..	Jasús ko kám
Estate	..	Mál matta, jhitti mitti
Estimate	..	Andázá
Estimate, (to)	..	Arkal káṭnu
Estimation	..	Samajh
Et cetera	..	Ityádi, ádi
Eternal	..	Sadai ko
Eunuch	..	Khokí, (khassi)
Even	..	Samma
Even now	..	Aile samán
Even, (adv.)	..	Pani
Evening	..	Beluka, sáṉjh
Evening, (in the).	..	Sám má, bhare
Event	..	Kurá
Ever	..	Kaile pani, (sukai)
Every	..	Sapai
Every body	..	Sabai
Evidence	..	Gawái
Evidently	..	Satya má
Evil	..	Dushṭa
Ewe	..	Bheṛí
Exact	..	Ṭhík, (twák)
Exactly	..	Ṭwakaí
Examination	..	Imtíhán
Examine, (to)	..	Jáṉchnu
Examiner	..	Jáṉchnyá

Example .. Napaná
Excavate, (to) .. Khopnu
Excavation .. Khaṉna
Except .. Siwái
Except .. Báṭo hernu
Exchange, (to) .. Sáṭnu
Excise .. Nasá
Excite, (to) .. Bhaṛkánu
Excited .. Antíyá
Excitement .. Garbar
Excuse .. Muáf, niuṉ, uttar
Excuse, (to) .. Chhemá g. muáf g.
Executioner .. Pone
Exercise, (School) .. Khata
Exercise, ..
(physical) .. Kasrat
Exhausted .. Sakye
Exhausted, (tired) .. Galye
Exhortation .. Upades
Expect .. Chháṛí
Expect, (to) .. Hernu, paunu
Expel, (to) .. Nikálnu
Expense .. Kharcha
Expensive .. Mahngo
Experience .. Thah, (tajurba)
Expert .. Sipalu
Explain .. Bayan garnu

Explode, (to)	.. Phuṭnu
Extend	.. Barayo
Extend, (to)	.. Baṛháuṉnu
Extent	.. Baraunu
Extinguish	.. Márnu, nibháuṉnu, bujhánnu
Extort, (to)	.. Jabarjasti linu
Extra	.. Fálṭo
Extract (to)	.. Nikálnu
Eye	.. Aṉkhá
Eye-brow	.. Áṉkhi bhuṉ
Eye-glass	.. Chasma, ('ainak)
Eye-lash	.. Parela
Eye-sight	.. Dirisṭi

F

Fable	.. Kaháni, kissa
Fabulous	.. Jhuṭhá, ṭhag
Face	.. Mukh, anhwáṛ
Facilitate	.. Sajilo banánu
Factory	.. Kárkhána
Failure	.. Harnu
Faint, (to)	.. Murchhá huṉnu
Fair, (just)	.. Sidho, sáncho
Fair, (colour)	.. Goro
Fairly	.. Nikai

Fairy	..	Parí
Faith, (religion)	..	Dharm
Faith	..	Patyáro
Faithful	..	Imándár, agiyakárí
Falcon	..	Báj
Fall, (to)	..	Laṛnu, khasnu, paṛnu
Fall back, (to)	..	Pachhi haṭnu
Fall, (down), (to)	..	Bhatkanu
Fall flat, (to)	..	Uttano
Falsehood	..	Jhuṭh,
False	..	Jhúṭhá
Falter	..	Bhak bhakánu
Family	..	Jahán, kulkutumb
Fame	..	Yas, kírti
Famous	..	Namí
Familiar	..	Janyá ko
Familiarity	..	Khulyá ko
Familiarise	..	Báni párnu
Famine	..	Aníkál
Fan	..	Náṉlo
Fanatic	..	Josilo
Fancy	...	Rucháunu
Fancy-sick	..	Prem ko bimár
Fane	..	Mandir
Far	..	Ṭáṛo
Fare	..	Tíro, (kiraya)
Farewell	..	Shubhamm, bidá

Farm	.. Khet, bárí
Farmer	.. Jimdár
Farrier	.. Ghoṛá ko nál lagánewálá
Farther	.. Lámo, agháṛí
Fascinate	.. Lalchánu
Fascination	.. Lalach
Fashion	.. Rítí
Fast, (Adj)	.. Chhito
Fasten, (to)	.. Kasnu, bádnu
Fasting	.. Upás
Fat, (n)	.. Boso
Fat, (Adj)	.. Moṭo
Fatal	.. Prán̲ mán̲rne
Fate	.. Bhág
Father (n)	.. Bábu
Father-in-law	.. Sasurá
Fatigue	.. Thakáí
Fault	.. Kasúr, (biránu)
Favour	.. Anugrah,
" (partiality)	.. Panpasáí
Favour, (to)	.. Ruchaunu
Favourite	.. Mukh laganu, nák ko bál
Fawn	.. Mirg ko bachchá
Fear, (n)	.. Tras, ḍar
Fear, (to)	.. Ḍarnu, (ḍaráun̲nu)
Fearful	.. Ḍar lágne
Fearless	.. Niḍar

Feast .. Kháná khanu
Feat .. Mauká ko kám
Feather .. Pwankh
February .. Phágun
Fee .. Bhárá
Feeble .. Kamzor
Feeble-minded .. Moto buddhi ko
Feed, (to) .. Khuwáuṉnu
Feel, (to) .. Tháhá páuṉnu
Feign .. Baháná, garnu
Fell .. Ḍhálnu
Female .. Aimai
Fence, (n) .. Báṛ
Fence, (to) .. Báṛ lagáunu
Fencing .. Báṛ
Ferry .. Ghát̤
Ferment .. Sodnu
Ferocious .. Nirdai, ujḍḍa
Ferocity .. Ujḍḍa paná
Fervid .. Jlyá ko
Festival .. Tiwár
Festoon .. Málá
Fetch, (to) .. Lyáuṉnu
Fetid .. Narámro khusbu wálá
Fetter .. Nel
Fever .. Táp, jaro
Few .. Thorai, kamti

Fiat	.. Ágyan̲
Fickle	.. Chanchal
Fiction	.. Jhúṭh muṭh ko
Fictitious	.. Banáwaṭi
Fiddle	.. Sárangi
Field	.. Khet, (for cultivation)
Field, (playing)	.. Maidán
Fierce	.. Jor-sor
Fifteen	.. Pandra
Fifty	.. Pachás
Fig	.. Nebharo
Fight (n)	.. Laṛáin̲ g.
Fight, (to)	.. Laṛnu
Fighting	.. Laṛáí
Figure, (numeral)	.. Ánkha
Figure, (body)	.. Áng, sarír
File	.. Reti
Fill, (to)	.. Bharnu
Fill in, (to)	.. Bharnu
Find, (to)	.. Páun̲nu, phela, bheṭáun̲u
Fine, (to)	.. Jaribáná garnu
Fine, (n)	.. Ḍan̲ḍ, jaríbáná
Fine, (Adj)	.. Rámro, masín̲no
Fine weather	.. Rámro din
Finger	.. Ángulá
Finger-nail	.. Nang

Finish, (to) .. Saknu, púro g, (bhyáunu)
Finished, (to be) .. Khatam, g.
Fire .. Ágo
Fire, (to) .. Fire garnu
Fire, (gun) .. Paṛkáuṉnu
Fire-fly .. Junkírí
Fire-place
(for cooking).. Chulhá, (chulo)
Fire-wood .. Dáura
Fire-works .. Átish báji
First .. Pahilo, pratham
First (of all) .. Sab bhanda pahile
First-rate .. Assal
Fish .. Máchchhá
Fish, (to) .. Machchhi márnu
Fist .. Muṛkí, (muṭṭhí)
Fit .. Máphik ko
Fit, (able) .. Láik
Fit, (adj) .. Ṭagro, Sanso
Fit in (to) .. Ṭhik bhai gayo
Fit, (to) .. Atáunu
Fitness .. Budhimati
Five .. Páṉch
Flag .. Dhajá, jhaṉḍí
Flame .. Juwálo
Flank .. Chheu
Flap .. Dhakkan

Flat, (adj) .. Chepṭo
Flattery .. Patyone
Flaw .. Khoṭ
Flax .. Sunpáṭ
Flea .. Upin̲ya
Fled .. Bhagi gayo
Flee, (to) .. Bhágnu
Flesh .. Shikár, másu
Fleet .. Beṛá
Flew .. Uṛeyo
Float, (to) .. Paurán̲nu, (bahnu)
Flock .. Bagál
Flog, (to) .. Betle piṭnu
Flood .. Barr, (bel), jalthal
Floor .. Majheri, bhúin̲
Flour .. Pítho
Flourishing .. Nikoánand
Flow, (to) .. Bahan̲nu
Flower .. Phúl
Flute .. Bánsrí
Fly, (to) .. Uṛnu
Fly, (n) .. Jhin̲gá, mákhá
Fly, (horse) .. Dáns
Foam .. Gáj
Foe .. Dushman
Fog .. Kuhiro
Fold, (to) .. Behernu

Fold, (enclosure) .. Khoṛ
Fold, (two-fold) .. Duguṉá
Follower .. Pachhí hiṭe chha
Follow, (to) .. Pachchhyáuṉnu,
pachhi jánu
Follow up, (to) .. Pichhá garnu
Food • .. Kháṉne thok, (khána)
Foment .. Seknu
Fool .. (Múrkha), anáṛí
Foolish .. Múrkha
Foot, (human) .. Goṛá, (páuṉ)
Foot, (i.e. on foot) .. Paidal
Foot-step .. Khaṭṭa ko awáj
Foot, (of hill) .. Phedi, Lakh ko chheu
Foot-mark .. Páielo ko nisán
For .. Lági, (lái)
Forbearance .. Sabar
Forbid .. Maná garnu
—God forbid .. Bhagwan na garos
Ford .. Gháṭ bhare ko
Ford, (to) .. Tarnu
Fore-arm .. Háth
Foreigner .. Pardesi or Videshi
Foreign .. Anyadesí, (pardesh)
Forest .. Ban, Jaṉgal
Forfeit, (to) .. Li haleu
Forgiveness .. Máfí, chhama

Forgive, (to) .. Chhimá, máph garnu
Fork .. Kán̲ṭá
Form .. Surat, Shakal
Former .. Agáṛiko
Formerly .. Pahile
Forsake, (to) .. Chhornu tyágnu
Fort .. Killa
Forth from .. Niskane báṭo
Fortified position .. Balliyo áṛ
Fortune .. San̲yog
Fortune, (good) .. Susan̲yog, (achchhá)kimat
Forty .. Chálís
Foundation .. Jag
Fowl .. Kukhrá
Fox .. Siyal
Fox, (black) .. Molsápri
Fox, (small) .. Phyáunro
Freckle .. Chhoyá
Free of cost .. Muphat, tesai
Fresh .. Álo, Tájá
Frequently .. Ghaṛí ghaṛí, bárambár
Friday .. Shukrbár
Friend .. Mitra, sangi, Joṛí
Friendly .. Sathi jasto
Friend-ship .. Sathi sangi
Fright .. Ḍar
Frighten, (to) .. Daráunu, tarsaunu

Frog .. Bhiágutá
From .. Báṭi, dekhi
Front .. Samne, (Adj) agáṛi, aghí
Front of, (in) .. Ko sámne
Frost .. Tusáro
Frown, (to) .. Mukh nichoṛnu
Fruit .. Phal
Fruitless .. Phal na bhae ko
Fruits .. Phalphúl
Fry .. Ghí yá tel má pakánu
Fuel .. Dáura
Fugitive .. Bhagoṛá
Full .. Bhariáko, bhari, bharye
Fulfil, (to) .. Purá garnu
Fulfilled, (to) .. Purá hunu
Fully .. Sabai
Fun .. Thatta
Fund .. Chandá, dán, (fund)
Funeral .. Mirtyu sanskár
Fungus .. Dhumsí
Funny .. Adad bhud
Furlough .. Razá
Further .. Ajha, aru, agari jau
Fur .. Nurm bál
Furnish, (to) .. Banaunu
Furniture .. Kath ko chij bij, álmál
Fury .. Gussa, risanu

Fuss .. Halla gulla
Futile .. Khállí, (bekár)
Future .. Áune, Ainda
Future, (in) .. Agbáṛi, ainda ko
Fly .. Chhi chhi, makha

G

Gain .. Naphá
Gain, (to) .. Paunu
Gale .. Áṉdhi, bhauṉri
Gall-bladder .. Pitta, pit
Gall-stone .. Patthri
Gallant .. Bír
Gallantry .. Bírta
Gallon .. *Gallon*
Gallop, (to) .. Phardáwál duguṛnu
Gallows .. Phaṉsí, jhundinu
Gambler .. Juwáṛi
Gambling .. Juwá
Gamble, (to) .. Juwá khelnu
Game .. Khel
Game, (shooting) .. Shikár
Gang .. Samuh, (ṭolí)
Gap .. Khulo jágá
Goal ... Jhelkháná
Gardner ... Málí

Garden	...	Bagaichha
Garland	...	Phul ko málá
Garment	...	Lugá
Garlic	...	Lasun
Gargle, (to)	...	Ghíghí garnu
Garrison	...	Kila ko palton
Gas	...	Gas
Gather, (to)	...	Batolnu, Jama garnu
Gate	...	Phaṭak
Gathering	...	Jámat
Gave	...	Diyo
Gay	...	Khus
Gaze, (to)	...	Taknu
Gazette	...	Gazette
Gear	...	Sámán
Geese	...	Haṉs
Gelding	...	Khasi
Gem	...	Lál, mani
Gentle	...	Bistari, bhala
Gently	...	Bistárai
General	...	Mukhya, bisesh
Generally	...	Bisesh gari
Generous	...	Dátá
Generosity	...	Dayáluta
Genii	...	Deo
Gentleman	..	Sáhib
Gentry	..	Ṭhulo manchhe

Genuine .. Aṣli, pakka
Germ .. Syano kiṛá
Germitate, (to) .. Umarnu
Gesture .. Ishara
Get, (to) .. Linu, páunu
Get away .. Jai jau
Get a chance, (to) .. Mauká pánu
Get down, (to) .. Tala utarnu
Get out, (to) .. Bhaira jánu
Get training, (to) .. Sikhláí pánu
Get tired, (to) .. Tháki jánu
Get loose, (to) ... Ḍhilo hunu
Get up, (to) .. Khaṛa hunu
Get asleep, (to) .. Suti jánu
Get back, (to) .. Pachhi jánu
Get drunk, (to) .. Nasha má hunu
Get home, (to) .. Ghar má pahuṉchunu
Get rid of, (to) .. Chhuṭi jánu
Get in, (to) .. Bhitra jánu
Get through, (to) .. Khatam garnu
Get off, (to) .. Nikálnu
Get together, (to) .. Sangai uṭhnu
Ghastly .. Murdá jasto
Ghee .. Ghiu
Ghost ... Bhūt, pret
Giant ... (Rashes), Deo

Giddy, (to be) ... Tauko ringáunu, bháuanau chaṛnu
Gift ... Dán
Gift, (in future) ... Pachhi ko dán
Giggle ... Khitkhiti, Haṉsnu
Ginger ... Aduwá, suṭo
Girdle ... Kamar baṉdh
Gird, (to) ... Báṉdhnu
Girl ... Keṭí, taruni
Girth ... Peṭí
Gist ... Ṭhik uttar
Give, (to) ... Dinu
Give an opinion, (to) ... Ráy dinu
Give away, (to) ... Jatánu
Give back, (to) ... Wápis dínu, ferkai dinu
Give in, (to) ... Hárnu
Give out, (to) ... Hári basnu
Give the hand, (to) ... Háth dinu
Give up (to) ... Chhoṛnu
Given, (to be) ... Di jána
Giver ... Dine wálá
Glad ... Khushi, ramánu
Gladden, (to) ... Ráji garnu
Gladness ... Ráji
Gladly ... Ráji le
Glance ... Najar

Glance, (to) ... Dikhái dinu
Glare, (n) ... Chamak
Glare, (to) ... Chamkinu
Glaring ... Chamke ko
Glass ... Shisá, aina
Glasses ... Ainak
Glass-ware ... Shisá ko bháṉṛá
Gleam ... Ujyálo hunu
Glide, (to) ... Áhiste-áhiste chalnu
Glitter, (to) ... Chamkinu
Gloom ... Aṉdhiyáro
Gloominess ... Aṉdiyáropan
Gloomy ... Dhumilo
Glorious ... Rámro, chamkilo
Glory ... Chamak
Glossary ... Khulyá ko barṛan
Glove ... Dastáná
Glue ... Gún
Gnaw, (to) ... Kutarnu
Go, (to) ... Jánu
Go away ... Jau
Goat ... Bákrá
Goat-skin ... Chhálá
Go out, (to) ... Boháira jánu
Go-over, (to) ... Pár jánu
Go through, (to) ... Síde jánu
Go one's way, (to)... Afno dhaṉg má jánu

Go-between ... Bích má jánu
Go-by ... Sang jánu
Go-down ... Tala jánu
Go across, (to) .. Pár jánu
Go forward, (to) .... Aghári jánu
Go on, (to) ... Jádai rahnu
Go off, (to) ... Jái jánu
Goddess .. Debí
God .. Parmeshwar
God-forbid .. Prameshwar na garos
Goitre .. Gánrá
Gold-smith .. Sunár
Gold .. Sun
Golden .. Sunharo
Gong .. Ghanṭá
Gonorrhoea .. Suják
Good .. Játi, rámro
Good, (moral) .. Bhalo
Goods .. Mall-haru
Good-bye .. Bidá
Goose ... Hans
Govern, (to) .. Ráj garnu
Governor .. Mukhiá, (láṭ sahab), jimwál
Government .. Sarkár
Gown .. Gawn
Grace .. Dayá

Graceful .. Dayálu
Graceless .. Kharáb
Gracious .. Dayá
Grade .. Darjá
Gradual .. Thoṛá thoṛá
Gradually .. Thoṛá thoṛá garera
Grain .. Dáná
Gram .. Chaná
Grand .. Ṭhulo
Grand-mother .. Bajai
Grand-father .. Báje
Grand-son .. Náti
Grand-daughter .. Nátini
Grand-child .. Náti-natini
Grandeur .. Chaṭak bhaṭak
Grant .. Bakhshish
Grant, (to) .. Dinu
Grant an application, (to) .. Arji manjúr garnu
Grant a request .. Kisí ko arzi lai manjur
Granter .. Dinu-wálá
Grapple, (n) .. Pakaṛ
Grapple, (to) .. Pakaṛnu
Grasp, (to) .. Pakaṛnu
Grasp, (n) .. Pakaṛ
Grape .. Angur, dákh
Grass .. Ghás, jhár, gháns

Grass, (tool for cutting) ... Ghás kaṭne haṉsiyá
Gratis ... Sitteíṉmáṉ
Grateful ... Guni
Gratefully ... Dhanebád chha
Gratification ... Sánṭo dino
Gratify, (to) ... Khushi g.
Gratitude .. Dhanebád
Gratuiotus ... Aseye diyáṉ
Grave, (n) ... Chihán
Grave, (adj) .. Gambhír
Gravity ... Sog surtá
Gray ... Phule ko
Graze, (to) (v. t.) .. Charáunu,
" (v. Int.) ... Charnu
Grazing ... Chari rahá chha
Grease ... Boso
Greasy ... Chiplo
Great ... Baṛo
Greatness ... Ṭhulo
Greatly ... Bahut ṭhulo
Greed ... Lob
Greedy ... Lobhi
Greediness ... Lob
Green ... Hario, hariyo
Green, (unripe) ... Káṉcho
Greet, (to) .. Ḍag dinu

Greeting	..	Sewá salám
Grey	..	Phusro
Grief	..	Dukha
Grievance	...	Dukh sukh, sato phernu
Grind, (to)	..	Pisnu, pinnu
Grin, /(to)	..	Khijánu
Grind-stone	..	Sán
Groom	..	Sais
Ground	..	Bhúin, bhui
Grow, (to)	..	Umrannu
Grow, (to), (increase)	..	Barhnu
Growl	..	Halla
Grub	..	Kháná, (food)
Grudge	..	Dushmani
Grudgingly	..	Naráj bhá chha
Grumble, (to)	..	Gangan garnu
Guarantee	..	Jamánat
Guarantee, (to)	..	Jamánat linu
Guarantor	..	Jamánat line manchhe
Guard	..	Chauki pahará
Guarded	..	Khabardár
Guardian	..	Jumebár
Guardianship	..	Jumebári
Guava	..	Amrud
Guess, (to)	..	Andáj garnu
Guest	..	Pahuna

Guest house .. Pahuna ko ghar
Guidance .. Baṭo bataune
Guide, (to) .. Baṭo bataunnu
Guide, (n) .. Baṭo bataune
Guile .. Dhoka
Guileful .. Dhoká dine wálá
Guileless .. Sada manchhe
Guilt .. Dosh
Guiltless .. Nirdoshi
Guilty .. Doshi
Guitar .. Bın
Gun .. Banduk
Gun-fire .. Banduk ko fire
Gunner .. Golandáz, top chaláne wálá
Gum .. Gonḏ
Gums .. Gigá
Gust .. Hawa ko jhoṉka
Gutter ... Baleni ko dhungro
Gymnastics .. Kasrat

H

Habit .. Báṉni, Behura
Habit, to make a, .. Behunra garnu
Habitable .. Basnu ko ṭhauṉ
Habitation .. Ghar

Habitual	.. Ádat garnu
Habitually	.. Barábar
Hackney, (carriage)	.. Kiraya ko gáṛí
Haggle, (to)	.. Jhagṛa fasad
Hag	.. Boksi, chuṛel
Hail	.. Asínná, (asínna paṛne)
Hair	.. Bál, Ráw, Kes
Hair, (Moustache)	... Jungá
Hair, (Hindus keep sacred lock of hair and the rest is saved)	.. Tuppi
Hale and hearty	.. Rámro, jati
Half	... Ádhá
Half-brother,	.. Sautilo bhái
Hall	.. Thulo ghar,
Halt, (to)	.. Paṛkhinu, ubhínnu
Halting place	.. Paṛáo mukam garne
Halve, (to)	.. Ádha ádha garnu
Hamlet	.. Sanu gaun
Hammer	.. Hathoṛá, mártol, ghan,
Hammer, (small)	.. Hathoṛí
Hammer, (gun)	.. Ghoṛá
Hammer, (to)	.. Hathoṛá piṭnu
Hammock	.. Jhulá jhulne
Hamper, (to)	.. Roki halnu

Hand	...	Háth, baháṉ
Hand-cuff	..	Hatkaṛi
Handful	...	Hátbhari, muṭhi
Hand-bill	...	Istihár
Handicraft	..	Háth ko bane ko
Handkerchief	..	Rúmal
Handle, (to)	..	Háth lagánu
Handle, (n)	...	Beṉṛ
Handwriting	..	Laikhni, likhai
Hand-mill	..	Jhaṉtho, (pitho pisne)
Handy	..	Najdik, kám ko chha
Handsome	..	Ramro
Hang	..	Jhundiánu, laṭkaunu
Hang	..	Phansi dinu
Hanging	...	Jhundayanu
Happen, (to)	...	Hunu
Happiness	..	Khusi
Happy, to be	...	Khusi hunu, khusi ramánu
Happy	..	Khushi, Ramáyo
Harass, (to)	..	Satánu
Harbour	..	Jaháj gháṭ
Harbour, (to) (ship)	...	Jaháj parkline jaga,
Hard	..	Sáro,
Hard, (tiresome)	..	Gáro
Harden, (to)	...	Sáro garnu

Hard up,	..	Paisa chhina
Hard-hearted	..	Saro muto
Hardly	...	Afthiyaro, kaṭhin saṉa
Hardship	..	Sáro dukh, saro muskil,
Hardware	..	Aluminium aur pital ko bháṛaṉ,
Hard work	..	Saro kám chha
Hardy	..	Bolyo, (majbut)
Hare	...	Khaṛau chokhṛi, (kharáyo, chaugarah)
Harlot	...	Pátar, besyá
Harm	...	Nuskán
Harm, (to)	..	Nuskán puránu
Harmful	..	Nuskán puráne mánus
Harmonium	..	Háth le bajáne bajá,
Harness	...	Ghoṛá ko jin
Harsh	..	Kaṛo
Harvest	...	Khetí káṭnu, bálí
Has	..	Sang—chha
Haste	..	Chhiṭo
Hasten, (to)	..	Chhiṭo garnu
Hat	..	Ṭopi
Hatch, (to)	..	Phúl kukṛá ko chhopnu,
Hatchet	...	Bancharo, (dawará chirne),
Hatless	...	Murulo
Hate, (to)	...	Narkhat garnu

Hatred	.. Narkhat
Haughty	.. Chhiṭo risane
Haul, (to)	.. Tán-nu
Have, (to)	.. Sangma, rakhnu
Have to, (to)	.. Paṛnu
Haversack	.. Jholá
Havoc	.. Na játi, Nás
Hawk	.. Bauṛái, Báj
Hawker	.. Bikri garnewálá
Hay	.. Sukhe ko ghás
Hazardous	.. Ḍar ko chha
Haze	.. Ṫuyánlo
He	... U
Head	.. Kapál, Ṭawko (animal)
Headache	... Kapal dukhe ko
Head long	.. Kapal ko bál
Headman	.. Jimwál, mukhya gaun ko,
Headquarters	.. Fauj bhaṉda pachhi basne ko jaga,
Head-rope	.. Aghári
Head strong	.. Mukhlágne
Heal, (to)	... Ramro garnu
Health	... Na rogi sarir ma,
Healthy	.. Ni rogi, niko
Heap	.. Dheri lagánu
Hear, (to)	... Kán le sunnu, sunnu
Hearer	... Kán le sunne wálá

Heard, (to be) .. Kán le sunai dinu,
Hearing .. Kán sunne
Heart .. Muto
Heart failure ... Dil chhorne
Heartless ... Dil ma hari na bha ko,
Hearth ... Chhuláh
Heartily .. Dil khusi le
Heart, (card) .. Pán
Heat .. Ghám
Heather .. Sanu sanu jhari
Heat-rash .. Ghamárá
Heaven .. Sawarg, sarga
Heaven, (sky) .. Akás
Heavy ... Garhuṉ, (garru)
Hedge ... Baṛ
Hedge grow .. Báṛ
Heed .. Fikr, Surta
Heel .. Kurkuchá
Height ... Lamu, ghare
Heir .. Gaddi ko málik
Held .. Pakre halu
Held up, (to be) .. Chheki dinu
Hell .. Narag, (Narka)
Helmet, (iron) .. Loha ko topi
Help ... Gohár
Get help, (to) .. Gohár pánu
Helpless .. Láchár

Helplessness	..	Láchárí
Helper	...	Sathi dinu
Hem	..	Magji
Hemorrhoids	...	Bawasir birámi
Hemorrhage	..	Ragat niskanu
Hemp	...	Bhang
Hen	..	Kukṛá ko pothi
Hence	..	Yo ṭhao baṭi
Henceforth	..	Kaile baṭí
Her	..	Yesko, usko
Herb	..	Jaṛi buṭi
Herd	...	Bákra ko reṛ
Herdsman	..	Bákra ko reṛ manchhe, gothálá
Here upon	...	Yetimáṉ
Here	...	Eta, (yaháṉ)
Here after	...	Isko pachhi
Hereditary	..	Marúsi
Hermit	...	Máta
Hero	...	Bahádur
Heroic	..	Bahaduri ko
Heroism	...	Bahaduri
Heron	..	Bákula
Hesitate, (to)	...	Hachki gayo
Hesitation	..	Samjhi bujhi
Hew, (to)	..	Kuṉdnu
Hiccough	...	Baruli

Hidden	..	Luke ko
Hidden, (to be)	...	Luknu lukánu
Hide and seek	...	Luka chupi khelnu
Hide	...	Chhálá
Hide, (to)	...	Luknu lukai dinu
Hideous	...	Na ramro
Hiding	..	Luke ko jaga
High	...	Sarai alko, (algo)
High handed	...	Jabarjasti garnu
Highlands	...	Lekh
Highlander	..	Sheshi
High-wayman	..	Chor chanḍál
Hill	..	Lekh
Hill-lock	..	Syanu lekh
Hill, (big)	..	Parbat
Hill side,	..	Kachhár, (daro tira)
Hilly	..	Pahari jaga
Him	..	Uslái
Hind	..	Murli, (pachhi)
Hinder, (to)	...	Roki dinu, (chheknu)
Hindrance	..	Roknu, thamnu
Hindmost	..	Sab bhanda pachhi lai thamnu,
Hindu law	..	Dharam sástar
Hinge	..	Kabjá
Hint	..	Ishará dinu
Hint, (to)	..	Sán, sankaunu

Hip	..	Phirpátá, kula
Hire	..	Kirayá
His	..	Usléi
History	...	Itihas, puráno kurá
Hit, (to)	..	Hánnu, márnu, Hirkánu,
Hitch	..	Sarde
Hither	..	Yetá
Hitherto	..	Aile aile sam,
Hive	..	Maha ko chhattá
Hoard, (to)	..	Batoli rakhnu
Hoard, (money), to,	..	Rupia jama garnu,
Hoarseness	..	Gháti basko
Hockey	...	Kath ko gola ko khel,
Hoe	..	Kodalo, khanne
Hoist, (to)	..	Janda mathi chhaṛhánu or lagánu
Hold, (to)	..	Pakaṛnu
Hold out, (to)	..	Suro bhaira samne garnu,
Holding		Jite ko
Hole	..	Dulo, bil
Hole, (made by people)	..	Chhcur
Holi	...	Tewhár
Holiday	..	Chhuṭṭi
Hollow	..	Khoklo
Hollow, (pit)	..	Ḍuṉgo, khokaro

Holy .. Pawitra
Home .. Ghar
Home, (at), .. Ghar má
Honest .. Kharo manchhe, imándár,
Honey .. Mahá
Honey comb .. Máh ko chhato
Honour .. Mán khánki, ijjat
Honour, (to) ... Khánki dinu
Hoof .. Khur pasúko
Hook .. Jhundánu, sán̲glo
Hook, (fish) .. Balsi
Hooligan .. Badmásh, luchhá
Hookka ... Bánse
Hop, (to) .. Uphárnu
Hoot, (to) .. Khái khái garnu
Hope ... Umed, (áshá)
Hope, (to) .. Umed garnu
Hopeful .. Umedwár
Hopeless .. Umed chhaina
Horde ... Toli
Horn ... Síng goru ko,
Hornbill, (bird) .. Dhanes
Hornet ... Bhiraya
Hornet, (small) .. Aringál
Horrible .. Hái hái
Hornet, (big) ... Bachhiu
Horoscope ... Janam patri

Horse	.. Ghoṛá
Horse-fly	.. Dáns
Horse-man	.. Ghoṛá ma chaṛne
Horse-shoe	.. Nál
Hosiery	.. Mojá
Hospitable	... Pawná ko khatir garnu,
Hospital	.. Aspátál
Host	.. Niuto dine
Hot, (water)	.. Táto
Hot, (day)	.. Niáno, ghám
Hour	.. Ghanṭá
House	.. Ghar
Hover, (to)	.. Nachnu, bhinbhinaunu, thirnu,
How	.. Kasari, kaso kasto
How much	.. Kati, katti
Howl	.. Karaunu
However	.. Tá, jauni parile pani,
Hug, (to)	.. Chháti má lagáunu,
Hunchback	.. Kubro
Hungry	.. Bhuk lagnu
Hunger	.. Bhuk
Hurt	.. Biraunu, choṭ
Hurricane	.. Adhi bhaunri
Hunt, (to)	.. Shikár khelnu
Husband	.. Logne
Husbandman	.. Kisáni, kheti garne

Hut .. Jhupro
Hyaena .. Bhápsilá

I

I .. M
Ice .. Hiuṉ
Idea .. Bichár, Samajh
Identification .. China jáni, chinda chha,
Idiot .. Murkha
Idle .. Sust, Alasiye
Idleness .. Alsi
Idol .. Murtí
If .. Yadi, Agar
Ignorant .. Ghámaṛ, murkha
Ill .. Birámi
Illness .. Bimárí
Illegal .. Niyáe ko birodh
Illicit .. Kharáb
Illegible .. Jo paṛhí jái sakdainá,
Illiterate .. Aṉpaṛh
Illustration .. Udáharan
Image .. Tharpaná kasi murti ko
Imagine .. Dhiyán ma lawuṉ,
Imitate, (to) .. Nakal garnu, khilli garnu
Immense .. Bahut ziáda
Immoral .. Pápí

Immortal	..	Amar, namarniyá,
Impartial	..	Niyáe
Imperfect	..	Ádhoro
Imperial	..	Ráj Sháhi
Imperil, (to)	...	Dukh ma paṛnu
Impertinent	..	Saikhi le bhare ko,
Impious	..	Nech
Implore, (to)	...	Arj garnu
Import, (to)	..	Báhir dekhin mál magaunu
Important	..	Jaruri kám
Impossible	..	Na-hunniyábát
Impotent	..	Na-mard
Impress	...	Chapa, nishan
Impress, (to)	..	Lubhaunu
Impression	..	Cháp
Imprisonment	..	Kaid
Improvement	..	Ramro g.
In	..	Má, Bhitra
Inaccurate	...	Galat
Inactive	..	Na bhawniya
Inattention	..	Láparwá
In the evening	..	Sánjh, Beluka
In the morning	...	Biháná
Incense	..	Dhup, risánno
Inch	..	Náp
Include	..	Milánu, lagaunu,

Including ... Samet, Sabai
Income .. Ámdaní, phaida
Incompetent ... Dukh diniye, nalaik
Increase, (to) .. Baṛháoniya, barhnu, (int)
Increment .. Tankha baṛhniya
Incurable .. Ṭhík na honiye
Independent ... Alag
India .. Hindustán
Indian .. Hindustáni, desí
Indicate, (to) .. Bataunu
Indistinct .. Ramro na nairiniye
Individual ... Akelái, akalái,
Indoor ... Ghar má
Industrious .. Mahintí
Industry .. Hunar, dastkari, háth ko kám
Inefficient .. Na-láik
Inexperienced .. Na-janiya
Infancy .. Bálakpan
Infant .. Náni, bálak
Infantry .. Paidal palṭan
" Indian .. Desi palṭan
" British .. Gorá palṭan
Infection .. Sarniya bimárí
Infectious disease .. Phailniya bimárí
Inferior ... Siyano kám
Influenza .. Sardi garmi ko tap

Information .. Samáchár, khabar
Inhale, (to) .. Sans bhitra linu
Inject, (to) ... Súi lagáunu, khopaunu,
Ink .. Masi
Inkstand ... Masi rakhniya bhanṛá
Inn ... Powá, bhatti
Inoculate, (to) .. Khopáunu
Insane .. Págal
Insect .. Kirá, kiraharu
Inside .. Bhitra
Insomnia .. Nínd na aoniya bimárí,
Instalment .. Kist lagáonu,
Instigate, (to) .. Bhaṛkáonu
Instruct, (to) .. Sikhaoniya kám garnu,
Instructor .. Kám sikhaoniya manus,
Instrument .. Auják, bájá
Insult .. Mán háni
Intellect .. Budhi
Intelligent .. Chalák, budhiwán
Intention ... Marji, irádá, ichá,
Intentionally ... Jání bujhera,
Intercourse .. Meljol
Interest .. Súd,biyáj, man
Interesting .. Manlái rucháoniya
Interrogation .. Sawál
Interval .. Thoṛá samai
Interview .. Bhenṭ

Intestines	.. Bhonsi ko antra
Intimation	... Samáchár
Into	... **Má**
Intolerable	.. Na sahi jane,
Intoxicant	.. Mad laone chíj,
Intrepid	.. Bahádur
Intricate	.. Muskil le samajh ma áor
Introduce, (to)	.. Bheṉṭ garaonu,
Invade, (to)	.. Dushman mathi chaṛhái garnu,
Invalid	.. Birámi
Invasion	.. **Dhawá**
Invention	... Naye bastu banaonu,
Inverse	.. Ulṭo
Invest, (to)	.. Rupia lagáunu
Investigation	.. Dekhbhál
Invisible	.. Ankha le na dekhene
Invoice	.. Mál ko hisáb
Iron	... Lohá, phalám
Iron-works	.. Lohá ko kárkháná
Irregular	.. Titar bitar
Irrigation	... Pání lagáunu,
Irrigation canal	.. Kulo, (nahr)
Is	... Chha
Island	... Ṭápú
Itch, (to)	... Chiláunu
Itch, (noun)	.. Luto

Ivory ... Háthi ko dánt,

J

Jackal ... Siyal
Jail .. Jhel
Jam, s. m., .. Áchár
Jam, v. t., ... Nichoṛnu
January .. Mágh
Jar .. Bháro, ghaṛá
Jasmine .. Chameli ko birwá
Jaundice .. Pinglo huniya rogue
Javelin ... Bhálá, barchí
Jaw .. Bángaro, bánra
Jay ... Tewa chara
Jealous ... Dáhí
Jealousy ... Irsha
Jest .. Thalá garnu
Jester .. Báṇṛ
Jewel .. Gahána
Jew .. Yahudí
Jew's harp .. Máchunga
Join, (to) .. Joṛnu, milánu
Joint .. Giṭhá, joṛ
Jointly .. Milkar
Joke .. Hansí, ṭhaṭṭá
Joy .. Anand, bhog

Judge	... Niyai garne ko afsar
Judge, (to)	.. Nisáphi, tharaunu
Judgment	.. Niyái garne ko hukm
Jug	.. Jug
Juggler	.. Bajígar
Juice	.. Ras, jol
July	.. Sáwan
Jump, (to)	.. Uphrinu
" , (down)	.. Phal ká
" , (over)	... Phál káṭnu
Junction	.. Milne ko tháoṉ
June	.. Asáṛ
Junior	.. Siyano
Jungle	.. Ban
Just, (ad)	.. Sidho, sancho
" , (Adv)	.. Aile, bharkar
Justice	.. Nyai
Justify	... Udrit batáunu

K

Keenness	... Tezí
Keen	... (Tez), tej
Keep, (to)	.. Rákhnu
Kernel	... Gudí
Kerosine oil	... Maṭṭí ko tel

Kettle	.. Baddhu, ketli
Key	... Chábí
Kick, (to)	.. Khutta le hánnu, láttle hirkáuṉnu,
Kid	.. Páthi
Kidney	.. Mirgula
Kill	.. Kaṭí dinu, márḍálnu
Kiln	.. Bhaṭṭí
Kin	.. Kuṭumba
Kind, (noun)	.. Kisam
" , (adj)	.. Dayá
Kindness	... Kirpa
Kindle	... Salkáuṉnu
King	.. Rájá
Kiss, (to)	.. Moai khánu
Kitchen	.. Bhánsa ghar
Kite, (bird)	.. Chíl
Knave	.. Thag, kapṭí
" , (card)	.. Gulám
Knead, (to)	.. Muchhnu
Knee	... Ghuṉṛá
Kneel, (to)	.. Ghuṉṛá ṭeknu
Knee-cap	.. Pángrá
Knife, (pen)	.. Cháku
" , (on kukri)	.. Karda
Knock, (to)	.. Khat khaṭaunu
" , (down)	.. Lotáunu

Knock down houses	.. Bhatkáuṉnu
Knot	.. Gáṉṭho
Know, (to)	.. Jánnu
Knowingly	... Jani bujmí kana
Know, (how to)	... Jánnu
Knowledge	... Tháha, bidhyá
Knuckle	.. Auṉláko gaṉṭho
Kookree	... Khukurí
Koran	.. Musalman haru ko sastra

L

Label	.. Chino
Labourer	.. Kuli, majdúr
Labourer, (field)	... Khetálá
Labour	.. Káj, kám
Laces	... Taṉá
Lad	.. Thito
Ladder	.. Lisnu, (síṛhí)
Lady	... Tarooni
Lake	.. Taláu, pokhrí
Lame	.. Dunro, Langro
Lamentation	.. Biláp
Lamp	.. Battí
Lamp, (earthen)	.. Diva
Lance naick	... Piut
Land, (to)	.. Utarnu

Land, (ground) .. Dhartí, (jamín)
Land, (country) ... Desh
Land-holder .. Jamíndár
Land-slip .. Pairo
Lane ... Sangro baṭo
Language ... Kurá, bhasa, bolí
Languor ... Dheruwá
Lap ... Kákh
Large ... Ṭhulo
Lark, (bird) ... Kurang kurang, chara
Last .. An̲t ma, ákhiri, pachhill
Last-year .. Gaya ko sál
Last .. Rahnu
Late, (noun) .. Dhilo,
Late, (to be) .. Derí le annu
Lately .. Dhilo gari
Latrine .. Ṭaṭṭí ghar
Laugh, (to) .. Han̲snu
Laugh, (at) ... Gijáunu, khisháunu
Law .. Ain
Lay-eggs .. Phul párnu
Lay-table ... Ochhyáun̲nu
Lazy, (adj) ... Lotey
Laziness .. Alchhe
Lead, (to) .. Doryáunu
Lead, (metal) .. Sísá
Leader .. Aguwa

Leaf, (tree) .. Pát
Leaf-let .. Patra
League .. Samáj
Leak, (to) .. Chunu
Lean, (to) .. Árish lagaunu
Lean, (over) .. Dhalkanu, jhuknu
Lean, (adj) .. Dublo
Learn, (to) .. Siknu
Least .. Sán̲nu, kam ko kam,
Leather .. Chhálá
Leave, (to) .. Chhoṛnu,
Leave, (farewell) .. Bida
Leech .. Juko
Left .. Debro, chryo,
Leg ... Khuṭṭá
Legend ... Sawái
Leisure ... Phursat, belá
Lemon .. Amilo, kagat
Lend, (to) .. Rin dinu
Length .. Lán̲mai
Leopard .. Chitwá
Leper ... Koṛí
Less ... Kamtí, ghaṭí
Lesson .. Arthi
Let, (to) (allow) .. Dinu
Letter, (post) ... Chiṭṭhí
Letter, (writing) .. Achchar

Level .. Samma, chepto
Lick, (to) .. Cháṭnu
Lid ... Ḍhakkan
Licence .. Parwáná
Lie, (a) .. Dhántkurá
Lie, (noun) .. Jhúṭh
Lie, (to) ... Dhántnu
Lie, down, (to) .. Ḍhalkaṉnu
Lift ... Uṭháunu
Life .. Jyan, sáns
Light, (to). .. Bálnu
Light, (int) .. Balnu,
Light, (n) .. Ujiyálo
Light, (in weight) ... Halun
Lightning .. Bijlí
Like this ... Esto
Like that ... Tyesto
Like, (to) .. Rucháunu, játi lágnu
Like, (Adj) .. Jasto
Lily .. Ek kism ko phúl
Lime .. Kamero, chun
Limp, (to) ... Khuchyáng garnu
Line ... Lahar
Lion .. Sher
Linseed .. Alsi
Link .. Sikrí
Lip ... Onṭh, (hoṉṭh)

List ... Bahi
Litter .. Kasingar
Little .. Siáno
Live, (to) ... Jiunnu
Live, (dwell) ... Basnu, rahnu
Liver ... Kalejo
Lizard .. Chhepáro
Load : Bhar, kumlo
Loan .. Rin
Lock .. Tálá
Locust ... Salan, salaha
Loft ... Machán
Log .. Muro, choiṭá
Loin-cloth .. Langoṭí, dhotí
Loins .. Chutar
Lonely .. Ekelai
Long .. Lánmo
Look, (to) ... Hernu
Look, (for) .. Khojnu
Loop .. Ghero
Loose, (adj) .. Khukulo
Loose, (to) .. Phukáunnu
Lose, (to) .. Haráunnu
Loss .. Nuksan, háni, nás
Lost (to be) .. Khojánu
Loud .. Charko, sáro
Loudly ... Charko gari

Louse	..	Jumrá
Love	..	Priti, máyá, prem, tith
Low, (adv)	..	Tala, undho
Low, (Adj)	..	Hoṉcho
Luck	..	Bhág
Lucky	...	Bhágemán
Luke-warm	..	Mantáto
Lump	..	Dallo
Lung	..	Phokso
Lustre	..	Chamkilo
Luxury	..	Mauj uṛánu

M

Machine	..	Mashín, kal
Mackintosh	...	Barsatí
Mad	..	Jhallá, págal
Magazine, (of rifle)	..	Purjá
Maiden	..	Taruní
Mail	..	Loguya ját
Maintain, (to)	..	Palan posan garnu
Maimed	..	Khurundo, gháyal bháyáko,
Main, (Adj)	..	Múl
Maize	..	Makái
Make, (to)	..	Banáuṉnu, garnu
Make, (a bed)	..	Bistar bichháunu

Make, (a noise) ... Hallá garnu
Male .. Jhánk
Mallet ... Mungro
Man ... Mánchha, (ádmí)
Mango .. Ám, ámp
Manhood .. Ádhabáins
Manner .. Parkár, rítí, dhang
Manure .. Mal
Many .. Dherai
Many people .. Dherai mánchhe
March, (to) .. March garnu, hitnu
March, (month) ... Chait
Mare .. Ghoṛí
Mark, (to) .. Chinnu
Market .. Bazár
Marmot .. Pia
Marry, (to) .. Biáh garnu
Marriage .. Biáh, (Byáhá)
Mars, (planet) .. Mangal
Marsh ... Dháp, shimshár, aul
Mason ... Ráj mistrí, gárokarmí
Mast .. Jaháj ko duro
Master .. Guru, swámí
Mat .. Mandro
Match ... Diyásalái
Matter, (Pus) .. Píp
Matter, (case) .. Bishay

Mattress .. Tosak, (gaddá)
Maund ... Man
May, (month) .. Jeṭh
Measles .. Dádura
Meaning .. Artha
Means .. Upáy
Measure .. Náp
Measuring rod .. Ṭáṉgo
Meat .. Shikár, másu
Medicine ... Okhadi
Meek .. Sudu
Meet, (to) .. Bheṭnu, phela párnu
Melon .. Tarbúj
Melon, (mask) .. Kharbujá
Melt .. Galnu, Paghalnu
Member .. Panch
Memory .. Sudhi
Mend, (to) . .. Banaunu
Mend, (patch), (to).. Tálnu
Mercy .. Chhimá
Merciful ... Dayalu
Message .. Samáchár
Mess .. Bhoj ko ṭháon, (miskot)
Met ... Milno
Metal .. Dhátu
Method ... Dhaṉg
Meteor ... Phutne tárá

Mice	... Musa
Microscope	.. Dúrbín
Micturate, (to)	... Mutnu
Midday	.. Madhyan, dopahar
Middle	.. Manjha, bích
Might	.. Sámartha
Mildew	.. Sinduri rog, dhumsi
Milc	.. Míl, (ádhá kos)
Military	.. Fauj
Milk	.. Dudh
Milk, (sour)	.. Dahí
Mill, (water)	.. ghatta
Millet	... Bhadu
Mina, (bird)	.. Dángre, saru
Minal	.. Dáphe
Mind	.. Man, buddhí
Mind, (to)	.. Dhanda, mannu
Mine	.. Mero
Mine, (coal)	.. Kháni
Mine, (military)	.. Surang
Minus	.. Kam
Minute	... Minaṭ
Miscarry, (to)	.. Tuhinu
Miser	.. Sum
Miss	.. Na páunnu
Mist	... Kuhiro, kuíro
Mistake	.. Bhúl

Mistress, (chief) .. Mukhiáni

Mix ... Missáuṉnu

Mole, (animal) .. Chhuchundro

Mole, (body) ... Kothí

Moment .. Chhin

Monday .. Sombár

Money .. Rupiá paisá

Mongoose ... Niolo musá

Monkey .. Bánar, láku

Monkey, (large) .. Dheruwá

Month .. Mahiná

Moon .. Jún

Moral ... Tapási

More ... Besí, jyásti

More-over .. Ajhai

More-people .. Aru mánchhe

Morning .. Bhiyána

Mortar .. Bajralep

Mosque .. Masjid

Mosquito .. Lámkhutte

Moss .. Jhyáu

Most .. Dherai

Moth .. Putli

Mother .. Ámá

Mould .. Sáncho

Mountain ... Lekh, (paháṛ)

Mouse .. Musá

Moustache .. Jungá
Mouth ... Mukh
Move, (to) .. Sárnu
Move, (to) (int) .. Hiṭnu
Much .. Dher
Much, (so) ... Yeti
Much, (how) .. Keti
Mud .. Hilo
Mulberry .. Kimu
Mule .. khachchar
Multiply, (to) .. Gunná, gunnu
mumps .. Hánre
Murmur .. Gangan
Muscle ... Nasá
Mushroom ... Chyán
Music .. (Git), rág
Musk .. Kasturí, kasturá
,, , (pod) ... Biná
Must ... Jarur
Mustard ... Rái
Mutiny ... Balwá, gadr
Muzzle .. Mohri
My ... Mero
Mystery .. Bhed

N

Naick .. Amaldár

Nail, (finger) .. Nang

Nail, (Iron) .. Preg, (kíl)

Naked .. Nángo

Name .. Náun, nám

Namely .. Arthát

Nape .. Ghichrá

Narrow .. Sánguro

Narrative ... Bayán

Nation .. Jati, kaum

Native .. Desí

Native-place .. Janmádes

Nay .. Nahín

Naval .. Bahrí

Near, (prep) .. Nira

Near .. Najík

Nearly .. Najdikai

Necessary (to be) .. Cháinnu

Necessity .. Zarúrat, cháhine

Necessaries ... Cháhineharu

Neck .. Ghánti, gala

Neck, (back of) .. Ghuchuk

Necklace .. Málá

Needle .. Siyo

Needy .. Kangál

Neglect .. Bisarnu

Negligence .. Besudh

Negro .. Kalo

Neigh .. Hinhináno
Neighbour .. Chhimeki
Neighbourhood .. Paṛos
Neighbouring ... Nagích ko
Nephew ... Bhatijá
Nerve ... Nasá
Nervous .. Harbar, áttine
Nest .. Gunṛ
Net .. Jál, jálí
Nettle .. Sisno
Never .. Kaile ne
New .. Nayá, naulá
Next .. Árko, dosro
Next-year ... Ághun
Nice ... Nakali, ramro
Night .. Rát
Night, (at) .. Ráti
Nip, (to) .. Chimátnu
Nip off (to) ... Chuṉṛnu
Nimble .. Phuṛtilo
No .. Hoina, ahaṉ
Nod, (in sleep) .. Jhulnu
Noble .. Sajjan
Noise .. Sabd, hallá
Nominal, (ad) ... Nam ko waste
Nominate .. Bharti garnu
Nonsense .. Anarth

Non .. Nahi
None .. Koi nahíṉ
Nook .. Kuna
Noon .. Do pahar, 12 baje din
Noose .. Pháṉsí
Nor .. Ani na
Normal ... Mámúli
North .. Uttar
Northern .. Uttar ko
Nose .. Nák
Nose-ring .. Buláki, mundro
Nose-gay .. Phul ko gucha
Nostril .. Nák ko dulo
Not .. Nahíṉ
Notable .. Parsidh
Notch .. Khoh
Note, (to) .. *Note* garnu, khayál garnu
Note, (curreney) .. *Note*
Notice .. Khabar dinu
Notion .. Bichár
Notorious .. Parsirdh
Nourish, (to) .. Pálnu
Novel .. Kahání pustak
Novice .. Chela
Now .. Aile, bharkar
Nowadays .. Áj-bholí
Nozzle .. Thuttnu, nák

Nude	..	Nangaí
Nuisance	..	Dukh dai
Numb, (to be)	...	Kakrinu
Numb, (adj)	...	Kakrio
Number	...	Gantí
Number, v. t.,	...	Ginnu
Numerous	...	Bahut
Nun	..	Bairágní
Nuptial	...	Bihá
Nurse	...	Daí
Nursery	...	Birwa ko ghar
Nut	...	Badám
Nut, (betel)	...	Pán
Nut, (used in betel)	...	Suparí
Nut-cracker	..	Sarotá
Nutmeg	...	Jáiphal
Nutshell	...	Chilká

O

Oh!	...	Tajub
Oak	..	Bánj¦ko rukh
Oar	..	Gabana
Oat	..	Jau
Oath,	..	Kariá, pashṭan
Oath (to take an)	..	Kasam khánu,
Obedient	..	Agiyá kari

Obedience	..	Agiyá palan
Obey, (to)	...	Hukum mánnu
Object	..	Chij, nisaná, matlab
Object, (to)	...	Padarth
Objection	..	Rokṭok, chhek thun
Obligation	...	Kar, níyam
Oblige, (to)	..	Kirpa garnu
Oblique	..	Chhatkyá
Obscene	..	Phohri, nanáuli
Obstacle	..	Badha
Obstinacy	..	Jid garnu
Obstinate	...	Magro, aṭṭeri
Obstruct, (to)	..	Rok
Obstruction	..	Rokáwaṭ
Obtain, (to)	...	Pánu
Obtained, (to be)	...	Milnu
Obvious	...	Partekcha
Occasion	..	Ausar
Occasionally	...	Kabhí kabhí
Occupation	...	Kar
Occupied	..	Lihalno
Occupy, (to)	...	Linu
Occur, (to)	..	Aiparno
Ocean	...	Mahsagar
O'clock	..	Baji
Octroi	..	Chungi
October	..	Kártik

Odd .. amel, falto, ekunthá
Odour, (good) .. Básin
Odour, (bad) .. Gandha
Of ... Ko
Off .. Máṉthi báṭo
Off, (gone) .. Gai, gayo
Off and on ... Kabhí kabhí
Off day .. Chhuṭṭi ko din
Offence .. Apradh, dukh
Offend, (to) .. Satáuṉnu
Offender .. Apradhí
Offer .. *Offer*, kimat,
Offer, (to) ... Kimat lagáunu
Offer, to (present) .. Bheṉṭ garnu
Offering .. Bheṉṭ
Office .. Daftar, *office*
Officer .. Afsar
Often .. Gharí gharí
Oil ... Tel
Oil man .. Telí
Ointment .. Mallam
Old, (people) .. Búṛho
Old, (things) ... Puráṉnu
Old, (worn) .. Thotro
Old-fashioned .. Puráṉne chál ko,
Omen .. Sagun
On ... Máṉ, máthí

Once .. Ek paltá, ek khep
One .. Ek
Onion .. Piáj
One-eyed .. Káná
Only .. Mátrai, (kháli)
Open, (to) .. Ughárnu, kholnu
Open, (to be) .. Kuli ko
Open air ... Kuli hawá
Openly .. Sáf sáf
Operate, (to) .. Operation garnu
Operation .. *Operation*
Opinion .. Mato, samajh, bichár
Opium ... Aphím
Opponent .. Dushman, beri
Opportunity .. Bela, mauká
Opposite ... Pári, sámnu, sáṉmuṉne,
Opposition .. Birodh
Oppress, (to) .. Dudh dinu
Or .. Ya
Orange ... Suntalá
Orchard ... Bág
Order, (to) .. Hukum dinu, arhaṉnu,
Order, (noun) ... Agyan, áin
Order, (to put in) .. Thankiaunu
Order, ..
(arrangement) ... Melo
Orderly ... Ardalli

Ordinary	.. Sadharan
Ornament	... Gahaná, jewar
Orphan	... Tuhurá, dáto
Other	... Árko, aru
Otherwise	... Nahita
Ought	... Cháhíṉ chha
Our	.. Háṉmro
Out	... Báira
Outstrip, (to)	... Uchhiṉnu
Outcaste	... Ját se báira
Outside	.. Báira
Oval	.. Lámchhe
Oven	.. Ageṉná
Over	.. Máthi
Over, (finished)	.. Bhaisakio
Overseer	.. Dafádár
Over-take	.. Phelá páṛnu
Over-turn	.. Ulṭáuṉnu
Over-hear, (to)	.. Sun linu
Over-load, (to)	... Jiyáda ládnu
Owe	.. Riṉ kárnu
Owl	.. Látá chaṛá
Own, (adj)	.. Áphnu
Owner	.. Dhani
Ox	.. Goru

P

Pace	.. Kadam

Pack, (cards)	.. Tás
Pack, (to)	... Poká paṛnu, thankiaunu
Pack off, (to)	... Rawána hunu
Packet	... Puntro
Pad	... Gaddi, f, gadda, m
Page, (of a book)	... Patrá
Pail, (wooden)	... Theko
Pail, (iron)	.. Balṭí
Pain	... Dukha
Paint, (to)	... Rangáunu
Paint	.. Rang
Pair	... Joṛá
Palace	... Rájmahal
Palm, (tree)	.. Tár ko rukh
Palm, (hand)	... Hatkelá
Palpitate, to	... Dhaṛaknu
Pale	... Pinglo
Pamphlet	... Pustika
Pan	... Kaṛahi
Pane, (glass)	... Sisa
Panic	... Ghabranu
Paradise	... Swarg
Panther	... Chituwá
Paper	... Kágaj, (kágat)
Paper-money	... *Note*
Papers	... Kágaját
Parachute	.. Chatri ko utarnu

English	Nepali
Parade	*Parade*, kawáj
Parallel	Barábar barábar
Paralysis	Bán
Pardon	Máf, (máph)
Parcel	*Parcel*
Parents	Ámábábu
Park	*Park*
Parlour	Gol kamra
Parrot	Shugá
Part	Bhág, aṉsha, hissa
Particle	Rati
Particular	Khás
Partner	Saṉgi
Partly	Ek chheu, ali ali
Partridge	Titrá
Party	Ṭolí
Pass, (to) away	Bitnu
Pass, (time)	Káṭnu
Pass, (outstrip)	Uchhiṉnu
Pass, (by)	Báṭo jánu
Pass, (permit)	Parwáná, purjá
Pass, (clearance)	Chalán
Pass, (mountain)	Gháṉṭí
Past	Biteko
Paste	Lai
Pasture	Kharka
Pat, (to)	Thapaknu

Patch, (to)	.. Talnu
Paternal	.. Bábu-ko
Path	... Górento, chorbáto
Patient	.. Rogí
Patience	.. Dhiraj
Patwari	.. *Paṭwárí*
Patron	.. Sahaek
Patrol	.. *Patrol*
Patrol, (to)	.. Gast garnu
Pattern	.. Namúnu
Pauper	.. Garib
Pause, (to)	.. Parkhanu
Paw	.. Panjá
Pay, (to)	.. Tirnu, dam dinu
Pay	.. Talab, tanka
Pay day	.. Tanka baṭnu ko din
Payment	.. Paisa dinu
Pea	.. Kerán
Peace	.. Sunsán, (sukh) mel, (laṛai na bhaya ko beta)
Peach	.. Áru
Peacock	.. Majur
Peak	.. Ṭipri
Pear	.. Náspátí
Pearl	.. Motí
Peasant	.. Gaṉwáṛ
Peg	.. Kíla

Pen .. Kalam
Penalty ... Jurmana
Pencil ... Pinsil
pension .. Pinsan
Penknife .. Chakku
Peon .. Chaprásí, *Orderly*
People ... Manchhe haru, (log)
Pepper .. Golmirch
Pepper-red .. Khursání
Per cent .. Saikaṛá
Perhaps .. Konı, sáyad, kunni,
Perjury .. Jhúṭ kasam
Permanent .. Tikan
Permission ... Ijájat
Permit ... Ijájat ko percha
Permit, (to) .. Ijájat dinu
Perplex, (to) ... Ghabranu
Persist, (to) ... Jid garnu
Persistent .. Jiddi
Person .. Admi
Personally .. Afai
Personality ... Mohani
Perspiration .. Pasíná
Persuade, (to) .. Phakáunu
Petition ... Arji, binti
Petrol ... *Petrol*
Petty .. Mamulí

Petal	.. Phul ko pat
Phlegm	.. Sigán
Physical drill	.. Akháṛá
Pick, (to)	.. Ṭipnu
Pick-axe	.. Gainti
Picket	.. *Picket*
Picture	.. Taswír
Piebald, (horse)	... Chhirbiryá
Pierce, (to)	.. Chheṛnu
Pig, (tame)	... Sungar
Pig, (wild)	.. Banel
Pigeon, (tame)	.. Parewá
Pigeon, (wild)	.. Malewa
Pigeon, (wild and big)	.. Bajewa
Pigeon, (green)	.. Halisa
Pile	.. Ḍher
Piles	.. Bawásir
Pilgrim	.. Jatri
Pilgrimage	.. Játra
Pill, (medicine)	.. Golí
Pillar	.. Khámbo
Pillow	.. Sirán
Pimple, (small)	.. Phoká, bibrá
" , (big)	.. Khatira
" , (black)	. Kothí
Pinch, (to)	... Chimatanu

Pincers, (crab)	.. Sanásu
Pine, (noun)	.. Sallá ko rukh
Pine-apple	.. Káble kuthan
Pipe	.. Nalá, nali
Pipe, (musical)	.. Morali
Pit	... Khálto, kháṛal
Pitch, (to) (a tent)	.. (Tambu) lagánu
Pitcher	.. Ghailá
Pity	.. Chhimá, dayá
Place	.. Ṭháu̱
Place, (very cool)	.. Shital
Place, (hot)	... Aul
Place, (to)	.. Rakhnu
Plague	... Ruṛhi putke rog
Plain	.. Maidan, sáf
Plains	.. Des, mades
Plaint	... Dáwá
Plaintiff	.. Sáhú, phiráte
Plainly	.. Sáf sáf
Plait	.. Bunnu
Plan, (to)	... Sochnu
Plan	... Naksa, rít, ḍháṉchá
Plane, (to)	.. Raṉdhnu
Plane, (n), (tool)	.. Raṉḍhá
Plank	... Phalyák
Plant, (n)	... Biruwá
Plant, (to)	.. Ropnu, gáṛnu, lagáuṉnu

Plantain	.. Kerá
Plate	... Thál
Platform	.. *Rail* ko *platform*
Platoon	... Platoon
Play, (to)	.. Khelnu
Player, (n)	.. Khelnewálá
Play ground	.. Khel ko maidán
Pleader	... Vakíl
Pleasant	... Ramáilo
Please, (to)	... Ramáunu, khush garnu
Pleased	... Ramáyo, (khushi)
Pleasure	.. Ánand, bhog, (khushi)
Pledge	.. Bandhak, wádá
Plentiful	.. Bahut
Plenty	... Bahut, saha, dherai
Plot	.. Yukti
Plough, (n)	... Halo
Plough, (to)	.. Halo jotnu
Ploughman	.. (Kisán)
Pluck, (to)	.. Ţipnu
Pluck, (noun)	.. Dhiraj
Plum	.. Álubokhrá, Álúcha
Plummet	... Sáhul
Plunder, (n)	... Lúţ
Plunder, (to)	... Lúţnu
Plunderer	... Lúţera
Plunge, (to)	.. Gotá lagánu

Ply, (to) .. Chalánu

Pneumonia .. *Pneumonia*, ek rog

Pocket .. Khati, (jeb)

Pod ... Bálá

Poison .. Bikh

Poisonous .. Bisálu

Point ... Ṭuppá

Poke, (to) .. Chhámchhum

Pole ... Ḍaṇḍá

Police station .. Tháná

Polish, (to) ... Chamkáuṉnu

Polish, (n) .. *Polish*

Polite ... Sushíl

Polo ... *Polo* ko khel

Pomegranate .. Dárim

Pommel .. Káṭhi, páṉgro

Pomp .. Dhúm dhám

Pond .. Pokharí

Pony ... Ṭoṭo, (ṭaṭṭu)

Pool ... Rah

Poor ... Kaṉgáli, nirdhani

Population .. (Ábádi)

Porcupine .. Dumsi

Possible ... Hosakne, huṉnu sakne.

Possibly ... Sáyad

Post ... Ḍák (mail)

Post, (to) ... Lagánu

Post, (stick) ..	Shito
Post, (a sentry) ...	*Sentry* lagánu
Posted, to be ...	Theknu
Postman ..	Ḍák batanuwálá
Post office ..	Ḍák ghar
Postpone, (to) ...	Ṭárnu
Pot, (clay) ..	Hánri
Pot, (brass or iron)...	Garuwá
Potato ...	Álú
Pouch for cartridge ..	Poch
Pour, (to) ...	Jháṛnu, khanyáunnu
Powerful ..	Balio
Power ..	Bal
Powder ...	Dhúlo (dust)
Powder ..	*Powder*
Powder, (fine) ..	Báruk
Practice ..	Sádhnu, mask
Precipice ...	Bhir
Pregnant ..	Bhári jyan, garbh
Prepare ..	Tiyár garnu
Prepared, (to be) ..	Tiyár h,
Present ..	Házir, (adj)
Present, (to be) ...	Házir hunu
Presence ..	Sánmel
Present, (noun) ...	Bakshish
Present, (to give) ..	Bakshish dinnu

Preserve .. Bachái rákhnu
Press, (down) ... Kháṉdnu
" , (urge) ... Ḍhipi láuṉṉu
" , (squeeze) .. Niṉchoṛnu
" , (printing) .. Chhápákháná
Press, (to) .. Ḍabánu
Pressure .. Dabáo
Prestige .. Ijjat, nám
Pretend, (to) .. Niuṉ, (baháná)
Pretence ... Niuṉ
Prevent ... Roknu
Pretty .. Rámro
Price .. Dám
Prick, (to) .. Ghochnu
Pride ... Miját
Prince .. Rája ko chhoro, rajkumár
Princess ... Rájkumári
Print, (to) ... Chhápnu
Printed, (to be) .. Chhapnu
Printing press ... Chhápakháná
Private .. Gupt (secret)
Private ... Ekántako
Probably ... Holá
Procession .. Barát
Profession .. Beopar, (trade)
Profit ... Naphá
Progress .. Baṛhnu

Promise, (to)	... Karahár
Promotion	... Baṛhti, (tarakki)
Proof	.. Pramán, sábút
Proper	.. Suwáuṉnu
Protect, (to)	... Jogáunu, bacháuṉnu
Protection	... Ṙakṣhe
Proud	.. Ghamanḍí
Provision, (food stuff)	... Rasad, kháne ko sámán
Provoke	.. Jiskyáuṉnu
Prune	.. Kalam káṭnu
Pull, (to)	... Tannu
Pull down, (to)	... Bhat káunu
Pulse	... Nárí
Pumpkin	.. Laukí
Punishment	.. Ḍaṉḍ, sazá
Pure	... Ṡudo, nirmal
Purge, (to)	... Jhára phirnu
Purge, (n)	.. Julab
Purple	.. Baijni
Purpose	.. Mansa, artha
Pursue, (to)	.. Pachhi pachhi jánu, khednu
Push, (to)	.. Ghacheṭnu, ṭhelnu
Put, (to)	.. Rakhnu
Put, (on)	.. Lagáunu
Put, (out)	... Jhiknu, bujhánu

Put, (to flight)	...	Bhagá dinu
Puzzle, (to)	..	Hairán garnu

Q

Quack	...	Anáṛí ved
Quail	...	Baṭer
Quarrel	..	Jhagṛá
Quarrelsome	..	Jhagarela
Quarter	...	Páo
Queen	..	Ráni
Queer	..	Anautho
Quench, (to)	...	Bujhánu
Quest	..	Khoj, ḍhúnḍ
Question	..	Sawál
Quick	..	Chhiṭo
Quiet	...	Cháṃchum
Quite	...	(Sarásar), syáṉṭṭhai
Quill	...	Pwánkh

R

Rabbit	...	Khaṛhá
Race	...	Hoṛábají
Race-course	..	Akháṛá
Rafter	..	Dáṉṛá, (karang)
Rag	..	Jhumro
Rage	..	Krodh

Ragged .. Tháṉgne
Raid .. Hawáí dhawá
Railway-line .. Rail ko líg
Rain .. Meh
Rain, (to) .. Barsanu
Rains .. Barkhá
Rainy-season .. Barkhá
Rainbow ... Indrení
Raise, (to) .. Uṭháuṉnu
Raisins .. Kismis
Ransom .. Daud
Ram, (noun) .. Bokya, sánde
Ram-rod ... Gaj
Rank .. Darjá
Rapid .. Beigi
Raspberry ... Aisálu
Rat .. Musá
Rate .. Bháo, mol
Rather .. Baru, jhan
Ration ... Rasad, (sidhá)
Ravine ... Kholhá
Raw .. Káṉcho, (kachchá)
Reach, (to) ... Samma pugnu
Read, (to) .. Paṛhnu
Ready .. Tiyár
Real ... Khara, (khás)
Reap, (to) ... Káṭnu

Rear .. Palnu
Reason .. Káran
Reasonable .. Uchit
Rebel .. Bidrohi
Rebellion .. Balwá
Rebuke, (to) .. Dhamkánu
Receive, (to) ... Páunnu
Recently .. Asti, alik din bhayo
Recognise .. Chínhnu
Recommend, (to) .. Sarkáunnu
Reconnoitre .. Khojihernu
Recruit .. Rangruṭ
Recruiting .. Galla
Recruit, (to) .. Bhartíjgarnu
Red .. Ráto, (lál)
Reflection .. Chháya
Refuse .. Kasingar
Regard .. Dhiyán
Regiment .. Palṭon
Regularly .. Barábar
Regular .. Ṭhik
Regulation .. (Dastur), niyam
Reign, (to) .. Ráj garnu
Rein .. Lagám
Release, (to) .. Chhoṛí dinnu
Relief, (in Army) .. Badalí
Relieve, (to) .. Sukh dinnu

Religion .. Dharm
Rely ... Biswás garnu
Remain .. Basnu, rahaṉnu, parkhaṉnu
Remainder .. Báṉki, ubryáko
Remedy ... Upai
Remember, (to) .. Samjhauṉnu
Remind .. Yád dilánu
Remit .. Dám diṉnu
Remove .. Lejáunu, sárnu, haláunu
Renown .. Kirti, nám
Rent ... Tíro, bháṛá, (kiráyá)
Repair .. Sájnu, (sudhárnu)
Repeat, (to) .. Dohráunu
Repeatedly ... Ghaṛí ghaṛí
Repent, (to) ... Pachhtáuṉnu
Reply ... Juwáp
Repose, (to) .. Bisrám garnu
Reprimand ... Ghuṛkí
Reproof ... Dhamkí
Repulse, (to) .. Hatai dinnu
Reputation ... Partistha
Request, (to) .. Bintí garnu
Request ... Bintí, nihedan
Require .. Máṉgnu
Reserve, (to) .. Rakhi chhoṛnu
Resolve, (to) .. Antnu, thaharánu

Reservoir	.. Haud
Residence	.. Ghar
Resident	.. Niwásí
Resignation	.. Tiyag
Resist, (to)	.. Roknu
Resistance	.. Atkao
Resolute	.. Pakká
Resource	... Sahara
Respect	.. Mán, adar
Respectable	.. Sajjan, mánwálo, (pujniye)
Respectful	.. Susheel
Responsible	.. Jimáwárí
Responsible, (to be)	.. Utara dinnu
Rest	.. Bishrám
Rest, (to)	.. Bisáunnu
Restless	.. Biyákul
Retire	... Pharki jánnu
Restriction	.. Bandhan
Result	.. Phal, nikás
Retreat, (to)	.. Pichaṛí haṭnu
Return fare	.. Lauṭno ko bháṛá
Return, (to)	.. Lauṭnu, parki ánu
Revenge	.. Palto, (badlá linu)
Reverse, (opposite)	.. Ulṭáulo

Revetment .. Parkál
Review .. Hernu, bichárnu
Revise .. Dohráuṉnu
Revolt ... Phúṭ, ráj bidroh
Reward .. Inám
Rhinoceros .. Gainra
Rib ... Kokha, (karang)
Ribbon .. Phitá
Rice, (cooked) .. Bhát
Rice, (parched) .. Chiura
Rice, (in fields) .. Dhán
Rice, (uncooked) .. Cháwal
Rich man ... Dhaní, dhan huṉne
Riches .. Dhan
Riddle .. Ahán
Ride, (to) .. Sawárí garnu
Ridge, (hill) .. Dánrá, lekh, ḍeṉ
Right, (hand) .. Dáhiná
Right, (not wrong)... Ṭhík
Right, (noun) .. Aktiyár
Rigorous, (rigid) .. Kaṭhor
Rim .. Kor, (kinárá)
Ring, (finger) ... Mundrí
Ring, (to) .. Bajáuṉnu
Ring-leader .. Mukhiyá
Riot .. Hullaṛ
Rioter ... Laṛáka

Ripe	..	Pákyáko, pákye
Ripen	..	Paknu, phulnu
Rise, (to)	..	Uṭhnu
Risk	...	Bhai
Rite	...	Bidhi
Rival	...	Bairí
River	..	Nadi
River, (small)	..	Kholá
Road	..	Báṭo
Road, (paved)	..	Saṭak
Road, (metal)	..	Roṛá
Roam	..	Bhaṭknu
Roar	..	Gúnj
Roast, (to)	...	Sekáuṉnu, polnu
Rob, (to)	...	Luṭnu, ṭhagnu
Robber	..	Ḍáku
Robbery	..	Chorí
Robe	..	Liwás
Rock	...	Shilápatthar, ḍhanr
Rod	..	Tángá, tangálo, lauro, laṭṭha
Rogue	..	Durjan
Roll, (to)	..	Bernu, lapeṭnu
Roll, (down to)	..	Palṭáuṉnu
Roller	...	Belan
Romance	..	Kaháni
Roof	..	Chhána

Room ... Koṭhá, kamrá
Root .. Jará, múla
Root, (to up) .. Ukhelnu
Rope ... Jiuṛí, ḍorí, sutari
Rope, (porter's) ... Námlo
Rose ... Guláb
Rot, (to) .. Kuhuṉnu
Rough : Khasro
Rough-ground .. Khaṛbaṛ
Rouse, (to) .. Uṭháuṉnu
Row ... Lahar
Royal ... Rájáko, rajasi
Rub, (to) .. Michnu, (malnu)
Rubbish .. Kasíṉgar
Ruby .. Rukhmani
Rude .. Anghar
Rug .. Kámlo, rári, pánkhi
Ruin ... Nás
Rule .. Ain, bidhi
Rule, (to) .. Ráj garnu
Ruler .. Hakim
Rum .. Rakshi
Rumour .. Jap
Run, (to) .. Dugarnu
Rupee .. Rupayá
Rush, (to) .. Ghusi jano
Rust ... Khíyá

Rusty .. Jang lageko

S

Sack ... Borá, thailo
Sacred .. Pabitra
Sacrifice .. Bali, balídán
Sacrifice, (to) ... Chadh , balídán garnu
Sad ... Udás
Sadness ... Udasí
Saddle .. Zín
Saddle, (to) .. Kasnu
Safe .. Nirbhai
Safely ... Kusallá je
Safety .. Bacháo
Sail, (to) .. Khenu
Sailor ... Kewat
Sake ... Lági
Salary .. Talab, (tankhá)
Sale .. Bikrí
Salt .. Nún
Salt, (adj) .. Nunílo
Salt-petre .. Sorá
Salvation .. Muktí
Salute, (to) ... Dhok garnu
Same ... Tyei, jastai
Sambhar ... Jaryáh

Sample	.. Bangi
Sanction	.. Manjur garnu
Sand	.. Bálua
Sandy-ground	.. Bálua bha ko bhúmí
Sarcastic	.. Tana, kalú
Satisfied, (to be)	.. Santusṭa
Satisfy, (to)	.. Agháunú
Saucepan	.. Táuli
Saturday	.. Sanicharbár
Saturn	.. Shani
Savage	.. Ghámaṛ, janglí
Savage	.. Banmánchha
Save, (to) (trans)	.. Bacháuṉnu
Save, (to) (int)	... Bachnu
Saving	... Bachaya ko
Saw	... Árá
Sawyer	.. Árá chalánewálá
Say, (to)	.. Bhannu, kahaṉnu
Scabbard	.. Khol, dáp
Scale, (of fish)	.. Katla
Scar	... Tátá, dám
Scare, (to)	... Daráunu
Scarce	.. Thorai
Scarcity	.. Kami
Scarlet	... Lal raṉg,
Scatter, (trans)	.. Phiṉjauṉnu
Scatter, (int)	.. Phiṉjnu

Scattered .. Titar bitar
Scissors ... Kaiṉchí
Scene .. Natak
Scent, (good) ... Básin
Scent, (bad) .. Ganda
Scent, (to) .. Suṉghnu
Scheme .. Upai
School ... Pathsala
School master .. Guru
Scholar .. Bidhyarthí
Scoff .. Ṭhaṭṭhá garnu
Scold .. Dhamkaunů
Scorch ... Istri ko dág
Scorn, (to) ... Ghin garnu
Scorpion .. Bichchí
Scotch .. Ghágre
Scrape, (to) .. Khurkaṉnu
Scrape off, (to) .. Táchhnu
Scratch .. Nagernu
Scratched, (to be) .. Chithranu
Scream, (to) .. Chichiaunu, chillaṉnu
Screen .. Chhirki, (pardá)
Screw .. Pech
Screw-driver .. Pech kas
Scurf .. Cháyá
Scythe ... Ánsi
Sea .. Sagar

Seaweed	... Simáli
Seal	.. Chháp
Sealing-wax	... Lakh
Search, (to)	... Khojnu
Season	.. Ritu, samay
Seasoned	.. Chhipiáko
Seasonable	.. Belá máphikko
Seat	.. Pirhá, pirká
Second	.. Dúsro
Secret, (adj)	.. Gupta
Secretly,	.. Luki luki
Section	... Bhág
Secure, (adv)	.. Nirbhai
Secure, (to)	.. Pánu
Security	.. Girbi
Sedition	.. Hullar
See	.. Dekhnu, hernu
Seed	.. Biu
" , (tea)	.. Geṛá
Seedling	... Biruwá
Seek, (to)	... Khojnu
Seem	.. Jasto h,
Seer	.. Ser
Seize, (to)	.. Samátnu, (pakaṛnu)
Seldom	... Kaile kaile máṉtrai
Select, (to)	.. Cháṉṭnu
Self	.. Áphai

Selfish	... Sawarthi
Selfishness	.. Sawarth
Sell, (to)	... Bechnu
Send, (to)	.. Paṭháuṉnu, (bhejnu)
Send, (for)	.. Buláuṉnu, paṭáuṉnu
Senses	.. Hosh, hos
Senseless	.. Behosh, behos
Sensible	.. Giyání
Sentence (judgment)	.. Hukm
Sentry	.. Pahará, senṭrí
Sentry-box	.. Gumti, ṭauwá
Separate, (to)	... Chhutáuṉnu, (alag garnu)
Separate, (adj)	.. Alag
September	.. Asoj
Series	.. Laṛí
Serpent	.. Sáp
Servant	.. Bándá, chákare
Serviceable	.. Kám yogeye
Settle, (to)	.. Basnu
Settle-price, (to)	.. Dám chukaunu
Set	... Rákhnu
Set fire, (to)	.. Ágo lagáuṉnu
Set out, (to)	.. Sidhárnu
Seventy	.. Sattri
Several	... Dherjaso
Severally	.. Alag¡alag

Sew .. Siunu
Shade ... Chháhári
Shadow .. Chháyá
Shady .. Chháyádár
Shake, (to) .. Halláuṉnu
Shallow .. Shím, janáre
Shame .. Láj
Shape .. Rúp, ḍawal
Share .. Ansa, bhág
Sharp ... Dhárílo, tikho, painu
Sharply .. Teji le
Sharpen, (to) .. Dhár lagáuṉnu, udhárnu
Sharpening stone .. Sili, sán
Shave, (to) .. Bál banáunu
Shavings .. Jhús
She .. U, tyo
Sheath .. Dáp
Shed .. Kaṭerá
Sheep .. Bheṉro
Sheet .. Chaddar
Shelf ... Khopá
Shell, (egg) .. Khapati
" , (gun) .. Golá
Shelter ... Áṛ
Shepherd .. Goṭhálá
Shew ... Dekháuṉnu
Shield ... Ḍhál

Shin .. Nalihár
Ship .. Náo
Shirt ... Bhoto, kurtha
Shiver .. Kámnu
Shock .. Dhakka
Shoe .. Juttá
Shoe-horse ... Nál
Shoot, (to) .. Goli le hirkánu
Shop ... Dukan
Shore .. Pákhá, kinárá
Short .. Chhoṭo
Short .. Kam, thoṛá
Shortly, quickly .. Alik dinmáṉ
Shot ... Chhará
Shoulder .. Kum, káṉdh
Shout ... Karáuṉnu, chillano
Show, (to) ... Dekháunu
Show, (noun) .. Baráti, ramíta
Shower .. Jharí, páni barse ko jhakora
Shrine .. Pavitra than, (mandir)
Shrink .. Sángrínu, khumchínu
Shroud ... Kafan
Shudder, (to) ... Tharthárauṉnu
Shut, (to) .. Thuṉnu, band garnu
Shutter .. Jhilmile
Sick .. (Bimár,) madhauro

Sickness .. Bimári
Sickly, (man) ... Rogí
Sickly, (plant) .. Sikro
Sickle .. Ánsi, haṉsiyá
Side, (hill) ... Chheu, tira
Side, (on this) .. Yeso
Side, (on that) ... Uso
Side, (on all sides)... Chheucháu
Side, (ribs) .. Kákhi, kokhá
Side, (to) .. Pakeh garnu
Siege ... Ghera
Siege, (to) ... Ghernu
Sieve ... Chalní
Sift ... Channu, (chálnu)
Sight, (gun) .. Makkhí, ḍig
Sight, (of eye) ... Najar, diresṭi
Sign ... Chiṉnu, (sanket)
Signal .. Sán, suchana
Signature .. Sahí
Signature, (to make) ... Lagáuṉnu
Silence ... Chup
Silent .. Gamílo
Silently .. Chuplagire
Silk ... Resham
Silver .. Cháṉdí
Similar ... Ak maphic

Simple	.. Sidá
Simply	.. Kewal
Sin	.. Páp
Sinner	.. Pápí
Since	... Báta
Sincere	.. Angiyakari
Sinful	.. Pápí
Sinew	... Nasá
Sing, (to)	.. Gánu
Singe	... Aile aile polnu, alik ḍaṛáuṉnu
Singer	.. Gawiyá
Single	.. Yota, eklo, eká
Single, (bachelor)	... Kanne
Singly	.. Ek ek garí
Sink, (to)	... Ḍúbnu
Sister	.. Didi, bahni
Sit, (to)	.. Basnu
Situation	.. Hálat
Sixth	... Chaṭwán
Sixty	.. Sáthi
Size	.. Ḍál, kad
Skill	.. Sip
Skilful	.. Sipálu
Skilfully	.. Chaturta le
Skin	.. Khálo, chálá
Skin	.. Khoseṭá (shells)

Skull .. Kapál
Sky .. Akás, sarga
Slap .. Thappaṛ
Slack .. Ḍhílo
Slate .. J̇híngití
Slaughter .. Káṭnu
Slave .. Kamáṉrá, dás
Slay, (to) ... Kaṭí diṉnu
Sleep, (to) ... Sutnu
Sleep, (noun) .. Nínd
Sleeve ... Báulá
Slight ... Kam, halko
Slip, (to) ... Laṛknu, chiphlíṉnu, (phisalnu)
Slippery .. Chiphlo
Slope ... Utar ḍhálu
Slow .. Ḍhilo, susto
Slowly .. Áhista
Slug ... Chiphlo
Small .. Syáno, chhoṭo
Smaller ... Bhanda syáno
Small-pox .. Biphar, máí, (shittá rog)
Smart .. Chatur
Smear, (to) .. Lipnu
Smell, (to) .. Súṉgnu
" , (bad) .. Gandha
" , (good) .. Básir

Smile, (to) .. Muskaránu
Smoke .. Dhuáṉ
Smooth .. Chillo
Snail .. Chiphlo kírá
Snake .. Lámkírá, sáp, (sarap)
" , (large) .. Agíngar
Snare .. Pánso
Snatch, (to) ... Khosnu
Sneak ... Khel halne
Sneer ... Hishknu, nák chaṛháunu
Sneeze .. Chim garnu, chiṉk
Sniff, (to) ... Súṉgnu
Snipe .. Cháha
Snore .. Ghurnu
Snow .. Hiun
So .. Yeso, tyeso, tyesto, yesto
So that .. Yeso bhayekole tá
So much .. Yeti, tyeti
So then .. Ta taba tá
Soap ... Sában
Sob .. Sisaknu
Sober ... Gambhir, saṉt
Society .. Samáj
Sod .. Chhapri
Soft .. Kamalo, (naram)
Soil .. Dhartí
Solder .. Ráṉg

Solder, (to) .. Ráṉg le joṛnu
Sold, (to be) .. Biknu
Soldier .. Tilaṉgá, sipáṉi, jawán
Sole, (foot) .. Paitla
Solely .. Aklai, kewal
Solicit, (to) ... Binti garnu
Solid .. Ṭhos
Some .. Koí, kyei, keti
Somehow .. Katai, kunai, parile
Sometimes .. Kaile kaile
Somewhere ... Kahíṉ, katai
Son-in-law .. Jawáin
Son .. Chhoro
Song ... Gíd
Soon .. Cháṉṛai, (as soon as-jasai)
Soothe, (to) .. Thap thápanu
Sore ... Gháo
Sort, (to) ... Chhánnu
Sort .. Kisam, rakam
Sorrow .. Shok
Sorry .. Udás
Soul ... Prán, (atmá)
Sound .. Sor
Sound, (to) .. Bajáuṉnu
" , (noun) .. Sabd
" , (good) .. Nirogi, niko, taugro
Sour .. Amílo

South	..	Dakhin
Sovereign	..	Maharáj
Sow, (to)	..	Biu chharnu, buno
Space	..	Thaun
Spacious	..	Phailiyako
Spade	..	Belchá
Spades, (cards)	..	Hukm
Spare, (to)	..	Bacháunu
Spare, (adj)	..	Phálṭu
Spark	...	Ágo ko chita, olení
Sparrow	...	Bhangera
Speak, (to)	..	Bhannu, (bolnu)
Spear	..	Bhálá, barchi
Special	..	Nij-bishes
Species	...	Jati, masálá
Specimen	..	Bangi
Spectacles	..	Chasmá
Speech	..	Bolí
Speed	..	Dháwá, (chal)
Spend	...	Kharchaṉnu
Spend, (time)	...	Káṭnu
Spider	..	Mákuro
Spill	...	Pokhnu
Spin, (to)	..	Bhurung ghumáunu
Spin, (thread)	..	Binnu, kátnu
Spinning rod	...	Katuwá
Spine	...	Daránlu

Spirit	.. Prán, sáns
Spit	.. Thúknu
Spite	.. Bair
Spleen	.. Tillí, phio
Splendid	.. Bharkilo
Splinter	.. Tukro, chirá
Split, (to)	.. Chirnu, pháṭnu
Spoke	.. Pakheto
Spoil, (to)	.. Bigáṛnu, biraunu,
Spoon	... Ḍáṛu, (chammach)
Sportsman	.. Shikari
Spot	.. Dhabba, Jagah, dág
Spotted	... Chhiribiryá
Sprain, (to)	.. Markanu
Spread, (to)	.. Phailáuṉnu
Spring, (to)	.. Uphrinu, phál kátnu
Spring, (of water)	.. Múl, jaruwápání
", (watch)	... Kamání
", (Season)	.. Basant
Sprinkle	... Chiṛaknu
Spur	.. Káṉṭa, (a horse)
Sprout	.. Ṭusá
Spy	.. Bhediyá
Squander	.. Gawaṉnu, nasht garnu
Square	.. Chár páṭe, chár kunne
Squeak	.. Chichíáunu
Squeeze	.. Ninchoṛnu, chepnu

Squint ... Serho
Squirrel ... Lokhroke
Stable ... Ghuṛsal
Stab .. Ghochnu, chhurí ḍásnu
Stag ... Bárásingo
Stage, (halting place) .. Bás, pod
Stagger ... Lotde lotde jánu
Stain .. Dág, dhabba
Stairs, (ladder) .. Lisnu, bharyáng, (sinṛhí), sawpan
Stale .. Bási
Stalk .. Dáṉṭh
Stall .. Kaṭerá
Stammer .. Bhagbhage garnu
Stamp .. Mohar, cháp, (ṭikaṭ)
Stamp, (to) ... Khuttá márnu
Stand, (to) .. Ubhíṉnu, tháro huṉnu, (khaṛá huṉnu)
Standing-order ... Chalyeko ain,
Standard .. Namunu, dhoja, (jhanḍá)
Star ... Tárá
Starch .. Kalap
Stare, (to) .. Táknu, ghúrnu
Start .. Hiti jánu, rawana huṉnu,
Starvation ... Uphas
State ... Gat

Statement .. Kathan, barnan
Statesman .. Nití jaunewálá
Statue .. Múrtí, partima
Stature .. Ḍíl
Stay, (to) .. Basí, rahanu
Steadily .. Sanbhlira
Steal, (to) ... Choránu
Steam .. Bháp, báf
Steamer .. Aganboṭ, jahái
Steel .. Ispat
Steep (up) ... Ukálo, (down) orhálo
Step, (to) ... Teknu, pag rakhnu
Step .. Pharká, ḍoro
Stick, (to) .. Uljhanu
Stick, (to), (in door) .. Alhhanu, atkanu
Stick, (noun) .. Lauro, chharí
Sticks, (small) ... Choila
Stiff .. Sáro
Still, (adj) .. Sunsán
" , (adv) ... Aile, ájí, shant
Sting, (to) . Toknu, sank márnu
Stingy ... Sum
Stir, (to) ... Hilánu
Stirrup .. Rikáb
Stitch ... Siláí garnu
Stock .. Punjí

Stockings or socks... Jurãb
Stomach ... Bhunnrí, peṭ
Stone .. Ḍunga
Stony .. Dungiyan
Stool .. Morhá, (chaukí)
Stoop, (to) ... Niurnu
Stooping .. Ghopto
Stop, (to) ... Chheknu, thámnu
Stop, (to be) .. Parkhnu, rahnu, uhbínu, arinu
Store ... Bhanṛár
Store-room ... Godám
Storey .. Talá, ánti
Storm .. Ándhí
Story .. Sawáí, katha
Straight .. Sojo, surílo, sarásá, (sidhá)
Strange .. Paráy ká, udekko,
Stranger .. Pardeshi, biráno mánchha
Strap .. Dhajji
Straw .. Parál, gháns pát
Strawberry ... Bhuinkáphal
Stray .. Bhaṭaknu
Stream .. Kholsi
Street ... Galí
Strength .. Bal, shakti, sámartha
Stretch .. Pasárna

Stretch, (legs)	..	Tankáunu
Stretch, (int)	..	Tanknu
Strict	..	Kaṭhor
Strike, (to)	...	Hirkáuṉnu
Strike, (o'clock)	...	Bajnu
Striking	..	Anokha
String	...	Rassí, dhágo
Strip, (to)	..	Nikhárnu
" , (clothes)	..	Kapṛe káṛnu
Striped	...	Dharkyá
Strive, (to)	...	Uddiyog garnu
Stroke, (to)	..	Musárnu
Strong	..	Balliyo
Struggle	..	Laṛnu
Stubble	...	Buchká
Student	...	Bidhyarthi
Study	...	Abhiyás
Stumble	...	Thokar khánu, ṭhes lagnu
Stupid	..	Ghámaṛ, murkha
Style	...	Dhaṉg
Subject	..	Parjá, (raiyat)
Subjection	...	Tábi
Submission	..	Adhinta
Subordinate	..	Agiya kàrí
Subscription	..	Chanda
Substantial	..	Pakká
Substitute	...	Badalí

Success	..	Phalít
Successor	...	Adhíkárí
Such	..	Yesto, tyesto
Suck, (to)	..	Chusnu
Suck in, (to)	...	Tutnu
Suddenly	..	Ek kási
Suffer, (to)	..	Jhelnu
Suffering	..	Dukh
Suffice	..	Pugnu
Suitable	...	Máphikko
Sugar	..	Chíní
Sugar-cane	...	Ukh, unkhu
Suicide	..	Atamghat
Sulphur	...	Gandhak
Sum	...	Rupiya paisa
Summer	...	Ghám ko din, (garmí)
Summit	..	Tiprí
Summon, (to)	...	Bulai paṭhanu
Sun	..	Súraj
Sunshine	..	Ghám
Sunday	...	Aitwár
Sunrise	..	Suraj-uday
Sunset	..	Suraj-ast
Superior	..	Sarest
Superstition	..	Jhuṭa dharm
Supervise, (to)	...	Dekh bhál garnu
Supply, (to)	...	Pahuncha̋nu

Support, (to help) ... Samálnu, (sambhálnu)
Support, (keep) ... Pálnu
Support .. Ţekan
Surface .. Gáro
Surely ... Sán̠chai
Surety ... Nischaye
Surpass .. Barhi jan̠nu
Surplus ... Baŗhti
Surprised, (to be) ... Chhakha mannu,
Surrender .. Pakará paŗnu
Surround, (to) .. Ghernu
Survive ... Ji rahan̠nu
Suspect, (to) ... Shanka garnu
Suspend ... Kuch samae ko alag kari dinnu
Suspicion ... Shan̠ká
Swagger, (to) ... Shekhi garnu
Swallow, (to) ... Nilnu
Swallow, (bird) ... Gauntelí
Swarm ... Bagál
Swear, (to) oath ... Kiriya khánu, kasam khán̠na
Sweat ... Pasíná
Sweep, (to) ... Baŗháŗnu
Sweep up, (to) ... Soharnu
Sweet, (adj) ... Míţho
Sweet, (noun) ... Míţháí

Sweetmeat	..	Miṭhái
Swell	...	Suninu, sújnu
Swift	...	Phurtilo
Swim, (to)	...	Tairnu, pairan̲n̲u
Swing, (to)	...	Jhúlnu
Sword	...	Tarwar (talwar)
Syphilis	..	Bhiringi

T

Table cloth	...	Mej ko chádar
Table	...	Mej, (mez)
Tahr	..	Jháral
Tail	..	Puchhár
" , (coins)	..	Chháp
" , (turban	..	Phurká
Take	..	Lin̲nu, lyáun̲nu
" , out	..	Nikálnu, jhiknu
" , off	..	Jhignu
" , in	..	Dántnu
" , away	...	Laiján̲nu, sarnu
Tale	..	Sawaí, kathá
Talk, (noun)	...	Kurá
Tame	..	Páliako, paluwá
Tank	...	Pokharí
Tape	...	Phita, (fita)
Tar	...	Koltár

Target .. Tárá
Taste, (to) .. Chákhnu, (sawadist)
Tavern ... Bhatti
Tax .. Rakam, sermá, kár
Tea ... Cháh
Teach, (to) .. Sikáun̲nu
Teacher ... Guru
Teak .. Ṭuní
Tear, (to) ... Pháṭnu, pháṛnu
" , noun .. Án̲su
Teat .. Kachono, thun
Tehsil ... Addá
Telegraph .. Tár
Telescope ... Durbín
Tell, (to) .. Bhaní din̲nu
Tell a lie, (to) .. Dhántnu
Tell the truth, (to) .. Sáncho bhannu
Temple .... Kapál
Temper .. Sobháo
Tender ... Káunlo
Tent .. Pál, chholdárí
" , pole .. Dandá
" , peg ... Mekh, kilo
Terrible ... Bhayának
Territory ... Khuwá, raje
Terror .. Bhaye
Testicle .. Gullá

Test ... Parikcha
Testify ... Gawahí din̲nu
Than ... Bhandá
Thank, (to) .. Dhaniyabád garnu, gun mán̲nu
Thank you .. Áphuká gun̲
That ... Tyo
Thatch ... Khar
Thaw, (to) .. Galnu
Their ... Tinako
Then, (at that time) .. Tyes bela
Then ... Tab
Then, so ... Tyes káranle
Thence .. Tyahan báṭo
There ... Uthá, tyahán
Therefore .. Yeskáran̲
There upon ... Tyetimán̲
These ... Yi
They ... Tí
Thick ... Moṭo, báklo
Thief .. Chor
Thigh .. Sánpro
Thigh bone ... Pásolá
Thin, (lean) ... Dublo
Thin, (adj) .. Pátulo
Thing .. Thok
Think .. Bichár garnu, sochnu

Thirst	.. Tirkhá
Thirsty	.. Tirkhá lagio
Thirsty, (to be)	.. Tirkháuṉnu
Thiṣ	.. Yo
Thither	.. Utá
Thorn	.. Káṉṛá
Thorough	.. Pakká
Thread	.. Dhágo
Thread, (sacred)	.. Rákhí (a string which Hindus tie round their wrist on the festival of Salano)
Threat, (noun)	.. Dhamkí
Threaten, (to)	.. Dhamkánu
Thrice	.. Tín khep
Throat	.. Ghánti, ghichro
Throne	.. Gaddí, (singhásan)
Throttle	.. Achetnu, saṉs thunnu
Through	.. Máṉjha báṭo
Throughout	... Bhari
Throw	.. Aphálnu, (phenknu)
Thumb	.. Buṛhi auṉlo
Thunder	.. Garja, gaṙaj, (kaṛak)
Thursday	... Bipaibár
Thus	.. Yeso
Tibet, (country)	.. Bhoṭ
Tick, (dod)	.. Kirná

Tidy	..	Ṭhíkṭhák
Tie, (to)	...	Kasnu, (bhandhnu)
Tiffin	..	Arní
Tiger	...	Chetwá, dharág, (sher) bágh
Tight	..	Sanguro, kaseko
Tighten	..	Kasnu
Tile	..	Jhiṉgiṭi
Till	...	Samma, jab samma
Time	...	Belá
Time, (season)	...	Samay
Time, (turn)	...	Phero, khep, bár, pálo
Tip	..	Ṭuppo, nok
Tiptoe	..	Panjá tekerá
Tire, (to be)	..	Thaki janu
Tire, (to)	...	Thaknu
To	..	Lái, tháni
Today	...	Áju, (áj)
Toe	..	Auṉlo
Toe-nail	..	Khuttáko nang
Title	..	Upadhi
Together	..	Sangai, ek saṉa
Token	..	Chinno
Tomato	...	Rámbherá
Tomb	...	Samadhí
Tomorrow	...	Bholí

Tomorrow,
(day after) .. Parsí

Tongue .. Jibre, jibro

Too, (adv) .. Sárai

" , (conj) .. Pani

Tool .. Hatiyár

Tooth .. Dáṉt

Top .. Ṭuppo, thápi, phurká

Torch .. Ranko

Torment .. Satanu

Torrent .. Chháṉgo, ganga ko bel

Tortoise ... Kachhuwá

Total .. Jamá

Totally ... Bilkul

Touch, (to) .. Chhuṉnu

Towards .. Tira

Tower ... Burj

Town .. Sahr

Toy .. Khilaunu

Trace .. Goho, pata

Track ... Páilo

Trade ... Beopár

Trader .. Beopárí

Tradition .. Kahávat

Tragedy ... Bilap ko sawang

Tragic ... Dukh dai

Training .. Kám sikhnu

Transfer	..	Badli
Transfer, (to)	...	Badalnu
Translate, (to)	...	Anubad garnu
Translate	...	Anubad
Translator	...	Anubadi
Transparent	...	Sangulo
Trample, (to)	...	Kuchalnu, (kuchal ḍálnu)
Trap	..	Dharap
" , small	...	Páso
" , big	...	Khor
Travel, (to)	..	Dulnu, (yatrá garnu)
Tray	...	Árhi
Traveller	...	Yatrí
Treacherous	..	Beimán, kapṭí
Treachery	...	Kapaṭ, (chhal)
Tread on	...	Kulchi di̱nnu
Treason	...	Rájdroh
Treasure	...	Dhan
Treasury	...	Dhansár
Tree	...	Rukh
Treat, (to)	...	Biyohár garnu
Treatment	...	Biyohár
Treaty	...	Sandhi
Tremble, (to)	...	Kámnu, (káṉpnu)
Trench	...	Kháwa
Trespass	...	Náṉghi pasnu
Tribute	..	Kar

Trigger	...	Librí, ṭrigar, (liblibi)
Trip	...	Ṭhes kháṉnu, (dawra)
Triple	..	Teharo
Tripod	..	Ohán
Trial	...	Nisáph, ajmáis
Trick, (to)	...	Chhalánu, ṭhagnu
Triumph	..	Bijai
Trouble	...	Bethá, dukha
Troublesome	..	Dukhdai
Trousers	..	Suruwál
Trowel	...	Khurpí
Trot	...	Kadam dugurnu
True	...	Sáṉcho, (sachchá)
Trumpet	..	Karnál, bogate, turi, (narsinga)
Trust, (to)	..	Bishwás, (bharosá)
Trunk	...	Madhus, (sanduq)
" , elephant	...	Suṉḍ
" , cut	..	Mura
" , tree	..	Phed, dhar
Try, (to)	..	Khojnu, kosish garnu
" , attempt	..	Mihnat
" , test	..	Jáṉchnu
Tube	..	Nali
Tuesday	..	Mangalbár
Tune	..	Rág, bhákha
Turban	...	Phitá

Turf	... Chaprí
Turmeric	.. Besár
Turn	... Ghúmnu
" , back	... Pharkaṉnu
" , (noun)	.. Bárí, pálo
Turns, by	.. Pálo pálo
Turtle	.. Kachhuwá
Tourist	... Báṭnu
Twice	... Dui khep
Twins	... Jaunlia
Twinkle	... Chamkánu
Type	... Ákár, chapa ko
Tyranny	.. Nirdayeta
Tyrant	... Nirdai

U

Ugly	... Kurup
Unadorned	.. Bucho, ríto
Unawares	.. Betháh, najándai
Udder	.. Thun
Umbrella	.. Chhátá
Unable	.. Ayoge
Unarmed	... Bina hathiyár ko
Unawares	... Bitháhá
Unceasing	... Lagátár
Unclean	.. Phohrí

Uncle	.. Mámá
Unconscious	.. Achet
Under	.. Talo, muni
Understand	.. Bújhnu, samajhnu
Undertake	.. Biṛá uṭháonu
Undo	.. Jhingnu, phukáunu
Uneasy	.. Biyakul
Uneducated	... Aṉpaṛh
Unemployed	.. Dhákre, pháltu
Unexpected	.. Achának
Unfaithful	.. Beímán, kapṭí
Unfit	.. Ayoge
Unfold	... Kholnu
Unfortunate	.. Abhági
Unholy	.. Apabitra
Ungrateful	... Nirguni, auguni
Uniform	.. Urdi, bana
Uniformly	.. Ekainánse
Union	.. Mel
Unite	... Saṉa joṛnu, phukálnu
Universe	... Sansár
Unjust	.. Anyáí, adharmí
Unjustly	... Unniyae
Unkind	.. Ḍust
Unknown	.. Aṉján
Unload	... Bhárí orhálnu
Unloyal	... Rájdrohi

Unluckily .. Anhoní
Unmarried ... Kunwaro
Unmerciful ... Hatiyaro
Unnecessary .. Befaida
Unpopular .. Luchchá
Unqualified .. Ayoge
Unripe .. Káṉcho, (kachchá), kach
Unsuccessful .. Nirás
Unsuitable .. Naphapne
Unite ... Phuskáunu
Untimely ... Besamaye
Unwilling .. Aman, birázi
Up .. Máṉthi, Umbho
Uphill .. Ukálo
Upper ... Máṉthillo
Upright .. Sedha
Uproar ... Halla
Uproot, (to) ... Ukhelnu
Upside-down .. Ulṭo sulṭo
Upset ... Bigáṛnu
Upwards .. Mástíra, máthi tíra
Urine ... Mút
Urge ... Thelnu
Urgent .. Awaseyek
Usage .. Retí
Use ... Kám
Useful .. Kámako

Useless ... (Raddí), berthai
Uselessly .. Suddhai
Usually .. Aksar
Usual .. Sadharan
Utensil .. Bhanrá
Utmost ... Atiyant
Utterly ... Bilkul

V

Vacant ... Khalí, suná
Vacation ... Chhuttí
Vaccinate, (to) .. Khopáunnu
Vaccination .. Bhed
Vain, (adj) ... Britta, suddhai
Valid .. Pakká
Valley .. Gairo, gahro, taráí
Valour ... Bahádur
Value .. Dám, mol
Valuable ... Amule
Various .. Waliwaliká, binna
Vane .. Patri
Vanish ... Alop hunno
Vanquish .. Haránu, jítnu
Vegetable .. Ságpát, tarkárí
Vehicle .. Sawárí
Veil ... Mujátro

Vein .. Nasá, rag
Velocity ... Beg
Velvet .. Maḵhmal
Venerable Buṛah
Vengeance .. Badalá, sánto
Venture ... Himmat garnu
Venus .. Shuk
Verandah .. Barandah
Verdant .. Hariyon
Verdict .. Bichárájná
Verdure .. Haryálí
Verification ... Ṭhík
Verify .. Ṭhik garnu
Very .. Dhere, baṛo, agghor
Vessel, (food) ... Bháṉṛá
Vest ... Bhoto
Via ... Báṛo
Vice .. Páp
Victory ... Jít
Vicinity ... Paṛos
Vicious .. Badmás
Victim ... Bali
Victor .. Bahádur
Victorious, (to be)... Jítnu
View .. Nimti
Village .. Gáoṉ
Vinegar .. Sirká

Vine	.. Angúr ko lahará
Violence	.. Bal
Violet	.. Baijní
Virgin	.. Kanya keti
Virtue	.. Pune
Visit, (to)	.. Darsan má jánu, bheṭ
Visitor	... Mulakati
Voice	.. Sor, sabd
Voluntarily	.. Aphaile
Vomit	.. Chhádnu, wák wák garnu, oknu
Vote	.. Bichár
Vow	.. Kiriya
Vulture	.. Gidha, gidh

W

Wag, (to)	.. Halánu
" , (noun)	.. Jhilkiyá
Wages	.. Talab, tankhawá
Waist	.. Kamar
Waist-coat	.. Áskat, bhoto
Wait	.. Parkhnu, parkhí basnu.
Wake, (trans)	.. Jagáunnu
" , (int)	.. Jágnu
Walk	.. Hinṛnu
Walk-about	.. Ḍulnu

Walking-stick	..	Lauro
Wall, (big)	...	Parkhál
" , (small)	...	Gáro, bhittá, (dewál)
Wallet	..	Bukchá
Walnut	..	Okhar, akhroṭ
Wander, (to)	...	Abáṭo lágnu
Want, (v)]	..	Mángnu
Wanted	...	Cháchíndo
War	...	Laṛáí
Warm	..	Táto
Warmth	...	Garmí
Warn	..	Chetáunnu
Warrant	..	Parwáná
Warp	...	Táná
Wart	..	Musá
Wash	..	Dhunnu
" , (bathe)	..	Noháṉnu
" , plates	...	Pakhálnu
Waste, (v. t.)	..	Bigáṛnu
Waste, (adv)	..	Nas
Wasp	..	Báṛulá
Watch	..	Ghaṛí, pahar
Watch, (to)	...	Chewá basnu, heri rahannu
Water,	..	Pání
Water-fowl	...	Pání ko kukra
Water-wheel	..	Ghata

Water-melon	...	Tarbuj, (tarbuz)
Water-fall	..	Jharná
Water-drain	..	Kholcha
Wave	...	Lahr
Wax	..	Lei, (múm)
Way	..	Pari
Way, (road)	...	Báṭo
Weak	...	Nirbal
Weakness	..	Nirbalte
Wealth	..	Dhan
Wealthy	..	Dhaní
Weapon	...	Hathiyár
Wear, (clothes)	...	Láuṉnu
Weary	...	Thake ko, thákye
Weasel	..	Neolá
Weather	..	Mausam
Web	..	Mákutá, jáli
Wednesday	..	Budhbár
Weed	...	Jhár
Weed, (water)	...	Simáli
Week	...	Sátá, (haftá)
Weep, (to)	...	Ruṉnu
Weigh, (to)	...	Jokhnu, taulaṉnu
Weighing-machine	...	Káṉṭá
Weighing-scales	..	Taráju
Weight	..	Bhár
Weighty	..	Garu

Well	.. Kuwá
" , (good)	.. Rámro
" , (healthy)	.. Niko
Well-done	... Shabásh
Welfare	.. Rájí khushí
West	.. Pachchhim
Westward	... Pachchhim ko oar
Wet	.. Bhijáuṉnu
Wet,-(to get)	... Rujhnu
What	:. Kye
What happened?	... Kye bhayo?
Wheat	.. Gahúṉ
Wheel	... Paiyá
When	... Kaile
When	.. Jaba
Whence	.. Kaháṉ báṭo, yaháṉ báṭo
Where	.. Kaháṉ, jaháṉ
Which	.. Kun, jo, jun
Whim	... Bahem
White	... Seto
White-ant	... Dhumira
White-wash	.. Chun láuṉnu
Whither	.. Katá, jatá
Whiskers	... Khátá
Whistle	... Swisata
" , (noise)	... Shusilo
Who	... Ko, kun, jo, jun

Whole	.. Sabai, singai
Whose	... Pátar, besyá
Why	... Kina
Wick	.. Saleto, dár
Wicked	.. Saitan
Wide	.. Gajilo, pharák
Widow	... Ránri
Widower	.. Ránro
Wife	.. Mukhenní, swáení
Wild	.. Jangalí, ban ko
Wild-dog	.. Boánsi
Wild-boar	.. Banel
Wildness	.. Jangalipan
Will	... Ichchhe
Willing	... Ráji
Willingly	.. Ráji le
Win	... Jitnu
Wind	... Batás
" , (to)	.. Ghumáunu
Window	.. Jhyál, (khirkí)
Wing	.. Pankh
Winnow	... Niphannu
Winter	.. Járo, hiundo
Wipe	.. Puchhnu, mitánu
Wire	... Tár
Wise	... Buddhimán
Wisdom	.. Buddhí

Wish	..	Ichchhe, man
With	..	Sita, sang, sana
Withdraw	..	Sarkanu
Wither	...	Oilhinnu, murjháonu
Withered	..	Skyáko
Within	..	Bhitra
Without	...	Bhaira
" , (alone)	..	Biná
Witness	..	Gawáí, sakchi
Witness, (testimony)	..	Gawáh
Wolf	..	Bheṛiyá
Woman	..	Ái mái, strí
Wonder	..	Ascharye
Wood, (for burning)	..	Káṭh
" , (forest)	..	Ban
Wool	..	Un
Woollen	..	Uní
Work	..	Káj, (kám)
Word	..	Kuro, shabd
World	..	Sansár, lok, jagat
Worldly	..	Sansárí
Worm	..	Aunsá, kirá
Worn-out	..	Thotro, ghise ko
Worship	...	Púja
Worshipper		Púјárí

Worthy	.. Yoge, máphik ko
Worthless	.. Raddí
Wound	.. Gháu, (choṭ)
Wounded	.. Ghaile
Wrap, (to)	.. Behernu, (lapeṭnu)
Wrath	.. Karodh
Wrathful	.. Karodhi
Wring, (to clothes)	.. Nichoṛnu
" , (hands)	.. Haláunu
" ,	.. Nimaṭhnu
Wreck	.. Nás
Wrestle	.. Kusti khelnu
Wretched	.. Abhoga
Wrist	.. Nari, ḍuṉṛulo
Write, (to)	.. Lekhnu
Writing	.. Likháí
Wrong	.. Anuchit, annye, (galti)
" , (error)	.. Bhúl

Y

Yard (measure)	.. Gaj
" , (court)	.. Ághan
Yea	.. Aṉ
Yawn, (to)	.. Hái garnu
Year	.. Barsha, sál, (san)
Yearly	.. Bárshik, sálenní

Yell	.. Chillaunu
Yellow	.. Pahenlo, pahilo, pinglo
Yes	.. Jyu, ho, an̲
Yesterday	.. Hijo
Yesterday, (day before)	.. Asti
Yolk	.. Kesar
Yet	.. Aile samma
" , (conj)	.. Tai
Yield	.. Dihálnu
" , (fruit)	.. Phal din̲nu
You	.. Timiharu
Young	.. Juwán
Younger	... Kánchho, (chhoṭá)
Youth	.. Jobhan, (jawání)
" , (boy)	.. Tarun̲
" , (girl)	.. Tarun̲í

Z

Zeal	.. Dhuni
Zealous	.. Man paryá ko
Zealously	... Utsah le
Zero	.. Sunne
Zig zag	... Tehṛo mehṛo
Zinc	... Jast
Zoological garden	.. Panchhi ghar (chiṛyá ghar)